GIL V

WITH BRIAN WHITNEY

RAW DEAL

THE UNTOLD STORY OF NYPD'S "CANNIBAL COP"

A MEMOIR

WILDBLUE PRESS

WildBluePress.com

RAW DEAL is a memoir and as such it is drawn on the recollections of the author and his interpretation of the events that impacted his life. Although the author and co-author have tried to convey these events, including conversations, as accurately as possible, and wherever possible documents are cited, this work is filtered through their eyes. There is no claim that others will recall these events in the same way.

RAW DEAL published by:
WILDBLUE PRESS
P.O. Box 102440
Denver, Colorado 80250

Publisher Disclaimer: Any opinions, statements of fact or fiction, descriptions, dialogue, and citations found in this book were provided by the author, and are solely those of the author. The publisher makes no claim as to their veracity or accuracy, and assumes no liability for the content.

ISBN 978-1-942266-84-6 Trade Paperback
ISBN 978-1-942266-83-9 eBook

Interior Formatting/Book Cover Design by Elijah Toten
www.totencreative.com

Publisher's Note

When Gil Valle and Brian Whitney approached us about publishing RAW DEAL, we were told that Gil wanted to tell his story "his way." Our concern was that "his way" included graphic descriptions of the sexual fantasies that landed Gil in hot water in the first place and included the abduction, torture and murder of women, as well as cannibalism. As with most of the general population, we find this sort of objectification and treatment of women, or any human beings, to be repugnant even as a "fantasy."

However, we also note, that such fare constitutes a large portion of the content of many thrillers and mysteries both in print and as film—the dubious distinction being that those are works of "fiction," as opposed to one man's online thoughts. It can also be said that writers and readers of true crime, as well as those who work in the television and film industry that portray real crime and criminals, rely on this sort of content for their occupations and leisure time. As such, we feel that moralizing about Gil's predilections to be somewhat duplicitous by anyone else who benefits from the depiction or description of criminal acts no matter how they attempt to couch it.

Yet, we may have still hesitated to publish this story, except for one sentence the authors included in their proposal: "When, if ever, does 'thought' cross the line and become a crime?" How many of us have ever thought about, or considered, an action that if made a reality would constitute a crime? Now what would you say if for having had that thought, but never having acted on it, the FBI or some other law enforcement agency arrested you at gunpoint in your home in front of your neighbors? And as a result, you lost your job and friends, and that your life became fodder for sensationalized media reports that made you an international laughing stock? And that you were then prosecuted, convicted and sent to prison? For a thought, a fantasy, a fiction.

In a free society that prides itself on the constitutional right to expression without government interference, it's a serious question that goes beyond Gil Valle and his online fetishes. What about the person who belongs to online terrorist groups but never commits a violent act? Or uses the internet to look up how to make a bomb out of curiosity? What about authors of thrillers and mysteries who Google criminal acts to add realism to their stories? At what point do we want law enforcement to be spying on us and at what point do we want them to act?

In other words, when, if ever, does a "thought" cross the line and become a crime? It is worth thinking about, and so we bring you **RAW DEAL: *The Untold Story of NYPD's "Cannibal Cop".***

"Good men with the misfortune of being aroused by socially unacceptable images carry a heavier burden than most; they must make do with fantasy, talk, or simulation, or they risk rejection, humiliation, and disclosure to third parties if they ask their partners to try or simulate some of their fantasied activities." –Dr. Park Dietz

PROLOGUE

The plan is coming along way better than I could have possibly imagined. For once, I found a guy to work with that handles himself professionally. I am getting tired of playing around with stupid bullshit.

We kept going back and forth on who it would be, but we finally picked out our target. She's beautiful, incredibly sweet, and vulnerable. She could not be more perfect for what we have planned.

There are always potential issues to worry about in a situation such as this, of course. Planning is of the utmost importance.

One potential problem is the fact that she knows me. She knows me quite well, actually. Considering she will be dead soon, this should not be much of an issue but still we will have to be cautious in our approach.

I met her in college and have known her for about ten years. We even used to hang out a bit from time to time. But so what? I will just use the fact that I know her to my advantage. She lives close by, all by herself. When I show up randomly at her place just to say hey, she won't even think twice about letting me in. "It's just me, your old friend Gil." Nothing to see here, nothing to worry about. Just open the door. She never found me threatening. Most people don't.

Of course, it is going to be an unannounced visit. We don't want anyone to know that I am going to see her. It is extremely important that, when she vanishes, my name will not be on anyone's lips. Once I get inside, I will say my "Hellos" and "How have you beens," then I will knock her out. Even this detail has to be planned, of course. If you try and knock someone out and don't do it right, then you are in a whole mess of shit right off the jump. I thought of using chloroform, but my partner suggested a quick shot to the neck with a stun gun to incapacitate her. I like that idea. It makes me hard.

Over time, we got the whole thing down cold. We planned out every single step. In excruciating detail, we talked about how we would make her completely disappear. No stone was left unturned, and every potential issue was discussed in order to cover our asses and to avoid detection by witnesses and the police.

The hard part is going to be getting her into my white van. Carrying an unconscious woman over your shoulder and throwing her in the back of a van tends to get a little attention. Not to mention that limp bodies are heavier than they appear. Once we get her inside the van, we will take her to my secluded house in the mountains that is about two hours away from her place. Once she is there it is going to be cake. The scene is totally deserted up there. Nobody is around for about a mile and a half. I spent the last several months converting the basement into a soundproofed torture chamber. I had a rotisserie apparatus measured out perfectly to her height. In the backyard, there is a large pit that we will use when it is time for the barbecue. She is going to wish she was never born. That part is going to be fun, but we still have a little work to do before we can start to enjoy ourselves.

I thought I was meticulous, but my partner has me beat. That dude is all over every little detail. He came up with all of the materials that we would need. We decided to go with zip ties and a ball gag to keep her quiet and compliant when she is in the van. If she wakes up before we got to the mountain house and causes us a problem, we will just keep her in line with the stun gun. Most people quiet down pretty quickly when the stun gun comes into play.

I have everything we need for the job. I picked up some pliers, a cattle prod, a blowtorch, a power drill, a flogger, and an electrical generator with alligator clips. I can't wait to see the look on her face when we have her chained up by her arms and I touch the two clips together and she sees that horrifying spark. The mechanical hoist to string her up is already installed and waiting for her arrival.

In actuality, she is a really cool woman. I always liked her. She always was so nice to me. I was nice to her too, of course, and that will help with the abduction. She has no idea who I really am and what I am capable of. She is not in the least deserving of what we are going to do to her. That makes it even sweeter, of course. We are going to water board her to start off with, and then get into some of the more heavy stuff. I imagine hoisting her up by her feet with her hands cuffed behind her back while we zap her with a cattle prod. The more she suffers, the better.

"This kid has no idea what is coming," he said to me.

Damn right, she didn't. It is about 2:00 o'clock on Tuesday morning right now. I love that she is probably sound asleep, drooling on her pillow, blissfully unaware of our plans. The whole thing is so ridiculously hot. I wonder what she is dreaming about, as we lay out the plan to kidnap her, rape her, brutally torture her, and then tie her onto the rotisserie and slowly cook her alive. With all our planning, we will almost certainly get away with it, but even if somehow we don't, doing this girl this way will be worth the years I will spend in prison. The sounds of her screaming and begging for her life will stay with me forever.

The kidnapping is obviously the most important part. Once her body is limp on the floor, I will text him and he will pull the van into her driveway. Then he will come in; we will scoop her up and place her in the back of the van. We'll be doing this at night so that we can use the darkness as a cover. It will only be a couple of seconds. Her neighborhood is quiet, so our odds are good. It is funny though, as much planning as we do, this part will all come down to dumb luck, but, if our luck holds, she will soon be in the van. I will get behind the wheel and start driving to the mountain house while he ties her up in the back.

His idea is that we should leave her clothes on and strip her at my place while she is awake. I am down for that. Her reaction will just add to our enjoyment. I am getting close now, as he describes how we will use zip ties to bind her wrists behind her back and her ankles together. Then he will stuff a rag or two in her mouth and bind it with duct tape. She will lay there asleep, bound and gagged. She will probably wake up at some point before we arrive, but that will be fine too. Watching her struggle and scream sounds kind of fun. My partner said during the ride he might not be able to help himself, and he might start off by sucking on her toes. He has a thing for feet. He said that while we cook her we should preserve her head, so that we could use it as the centerpiece of the table while we devoured the rest of her barbecued body.

I imagine the scene. I picture her bound and gagged, I picture her strung up by her ankles, I think of her tied onto a rotisserie screaming for her life as we turn her over a low fire.

Then I get off and go to bed. Maybe tomorrow we'll start another story.

1.

I know that in a book about the life of the Cannibal Cop you probably don't care much about my childhood. Unless there was some traumatic, horrifying event that could have contributed to turning me into the monster that everyone read about after I was arrested, who really cares how I grew up?

Something had to have happened, right? How did a police officer, from a nice family, turn into someone that had really wild, and, to most, deplorable fantasies about torture and cannibalism? What was the moment in his childhood that inspired everything?

Since my life was turned upside down, I have been asked questions like these a lot. I hate to be the bearer of bad news, but nothing in my childhood was the inspiration for my kink. I didn't start random fires or torture animals. I wasn't violent. I didn't wet the bed well into my teens.

It was quite the contrary actually. I grew up in a quiet, safe neighborhood in Queens, New York, where, for the most part, nothing ever happened. In my childhood there were a lot of trips to theme parks, I had plenty of friends, I was popular in school, I got good grades, and I played a whole lot of baseball.

My parents didn't get along all that well though. There were very rare instances I can think of where my parents were able to get along like a normal husband and wife. Most of the time they were fighting. The rule of thumb was that if they weren't arguing about something, they weren't talking at all. They separated in 1989, when I was five years old.

I would have preferred to have grown up in a home where my mother and father loved each other, but that's not how it worked out. That being said, both of my parents were very much a part of my upbringing. They loved me. They both were affectionate and hugged me a lot when I was young. My current motivation to push hard and succeed at any challenge in front of me is my father's influence. My soft spot for the unfortunate, my love of animals, and my overall kindness and generosity comes from my mother.

For much of my elementary school days I was incredibly shy. I was pretty good at making friends one on one but I was deathly afraid of public speaking. Standing in front of the class reading a book report or just reading aloud from the textbook gave me that really nervous feeling in my stomach. People who know me today would not believe how shy I was back then. I would occasionally stutter, but fortunately, I was never made fun of.

My shyness extended to girls. I never had a problem approaching a girl or talking to her, but if I had a crush on a girl I rarely had the balls to tell her that I liked her or make a move. What moves could you really make in elementary school though?

As a kid I was really into baseball. We had one of those Dwight Gooden pitching machines in the apartment when I was three years old. My father would put a whiffle ball into the machine and it would fire a pitch at me. While my father was at work, before I started school, my mother would take me to the park with the bat and whiffle ball and pitch to me. I was hooked.

My father had two TVs on every night, one right next to the other. During baseball season, the Yankees would be on one TV and the Mets on the second. He was a Yankees fan so, naturally, I followed along, but he always got more joy out of the Mets losing than the Yankees winning. I was taught to make fun of the Mets and their fans; it became one of our favorite pastimes together.

We would go to games together at Yankee stadium and I loved them. The green grass, the stadium sounds, and the crack of the bat, it all mesmerized me. I loved the voice of Bob Sheppard, the PA announcer. I was starting to get a passion for the game, and I finally began playing organized baseball at the age of nine. They passed out flyers one day in second grade, encouraging us to sign up for the Forest Hills Little League. I showed it to my father when I got home and he signed me right up. For the rest of my school career baseball was a big thing for me.

I was a natural and was good right away. With success came pressure though. Not only was I hard on myself, but my dad was hard on me too. Just as I didn't want to disappoint him with academics, I didn't want to disappoint him on the field. Unfortunately, the older and better I got, the more pressure I felt. There were times I prayed that the ball wouldn't be hit to me so that I wouldn't have the chance to screw it up.

It is around this time in life that most boys start getting sexual feelings for the first time. I was eleven years old or so, and I was no different. Well, I was a bit different I suppose, because I started getting turned on by bondage and S & M stuff. As I said earlier, I don't have a stunning revelation about why this happened. I didn't choose it. It was just there. I would see images or video clips on TV or in a movie of women being tied up and helpless and I would get turned on. It excited me.

Someone's sexual orientation is what the professionals in the field call "fixed". In other words, if you are gay, you don't simply choose to be gay., If you get turned on by feet, it isn't like you just woke up one day and decided that feet were your thing, and if you get hard when you see a woman tied up on a platter, then there is not a whole lot you can do to change that. I've done a lot of reading about sexuality and paraphilias over the past few years. A major misconception is that people who have a fetish choose to be aroused by that, and that if a person has an odd fetish, he or she must have some kind of moral problem. That's not how it works.

And why would anyone care to change it anyway? The way I was sexually, and what turned me on, was never anything I thought a whole lot about. It just was what it was. I didn't spend any time worrying about it. It was just a place I went to in my head. No one would ever know, so I never considered it a problem. I was the person that I was, and as far as I was concerned, that was okay.

There were three girls I was seriously attracted to in junior high school. When I masturbated and thought about them, I would imagine them tied up. There were never really any other characters involved in the scenarios. I didn't think of myself tying them up, or other people tying them up. An image would just come into my mind of the girl tied up. They would never be naked, just wearing a school uniform, or maybe a bathing suit. They might struggle a bit, they might be quiet and lie there, but they were always tied up.

When I was fourteen, I started my first year at Archbishop Molloy High School. While trying to decide where to go to school, I thought to myself, if I was serious about baseball,

I would go to Molloy, if I wanted to have fun with girls, I would go to one of Molloy's rival schools, St. Francis Prep. I ended up at Molloy on a partial academic scholarship and made the baseball team.

Baseball continued to be a large part of my life. During the summer, when school was out, I played a lot of baseball for a team called the Cardinals. We were on the road a lot, playing tournaments all up and down the east coast. Cardinal games were pressure packed and rarely fun for me. I liked baseball because I was good at it, but way too many people around me took it too seriously. The coaches and parents were nuts. One time, my father almost came to blows with another parent who was about twice his size over something that happened during a game. One of the coaches yelled at us if we beat an inferior team in a relatively close game. That's right, we were screamed at and berated for not beating a team badly enough.

That was life in the late 1990s. Then I discovered America Online. Almost immediately, I got into the internet and all it had to offer. It was love at first sight. I thought it was so cool, right from my bedroom, to be able to look up baseball stats just like that and to have the capability to chat with anyone in the world. We had this huge, bright orange iMac with the old school dial-up connection. I started to get into the whole chat and instant message thing, and would, on occasion, chat with random strangers in public chat rooms. I soon realized that I could say whatever I wanted and be whoever I wanted. I would get in chat rooms and talk to girls when I could. At least, they said they were girls. Who knows who they really were?

I never considered meeting any of the people I was chatting with. It never crossed my mind. I was curious about them though. I liked chatting with people from other parts of the country, and learning what they were interested in. Sometimes I would find myself making up or embellishing details about who I was. I was a good baseball player, but I'd talk about how I was the best player in the city. I would sometimes flaunt around fake wealth. I realized I could be whoever I wanted to be on there and there was no way anything I said could be verified. I thought that was pretty cool.

Like most kids my age, my discovery of the Internet led to my first experiences with porn. I don't remember the first porn site I looked at, but just like what was going on in my head, I was mostly interested in pictures of women in bondage. I would get way more excited seeing a hot woman tied up with a gag in her mouth, even if she had clothes on, than looking at the same hot woman naked and unrestrained.

For a kid, the sites I found seemed kind of wild, but looking back on it, these were just really vanilla bondage sites and pictures that I looked at. They weren't violent or particularly sadistic, just women naked and tied up; hogtied, tied down to a bed, things of that nature. If I saw a picture I liked, I would think about a girl I knew and I'd imagine her in that situation.

My friends talked about porn sites they looked at, which were just your typical guy and girl fucking kind of thing. I would play along, but I never told them about the bondage sites that I liked to check out. I figured they would bust my balls relentlessly and think I was some kind of freak. I didn't think it was the kind of thing I wanted to advertise. Don't get me wrong. I didn't feel like a freak about it, I just had that sense of self-preservation that every kid has when they like something vastly different than their friends.

Try and imagine that your sex drive is focused on tying women up, seeing them helpless, having them naked on a platter before you. If you didn't want to volunteer that it would be the kind of thing you kept to yourself. You aren't going to tell your wife about it. You aren't going to tell your friends or go out for some beers with the guys at work and say, "I have to tell you, Joe, I find naked women that are tied up with apples in their mouths extremely erotic, and I feel really bad about it." You aren't going to tell anyone. Not anyone you know in real life anyway.

Being involved in athletics and other extracurricular activities afforded me the chance to mingle with some of the girls after normal school hours. I gravitated towards some of the female athletes and on one of these random excursions I approached the point guard of the girls' basketball team. Everyone remembers the first person they fell in love with. For me, it was in late autumn of the year 2000, when I was sixteen. Her name was Melanie and boy, did I fall hard.

We chatted briefly that first day in the hallway, and ended up taking the subway together where I got her phone number. In the coming days and weeks, I couldn't stop thinking about her. I had it bad. She was by no means the prettiest girl in school, in fact, she rarely ever wore makeup, but I liked that about her. She was a freckle-faced Irish girl who was comfortable being herself and just wearing a ponytail every single day.

She told me early on that she wasn't interested in a boyfriend, but she also told me she was interested in hanging out. This began the beginning of my confusion around her. We hung out for the first time on a cold Saturday afternoon. I met her at Molloy after her basketball practice. We went to a local bagel place and then saw *The Gift*, a movie with Cate

Blanchett, Keanu Reeves, and Katie Holmes. We ended the day at my mother's house where we watched college basketball until her mother came to pick her up. It was a very low key and comfortable first day. I wanted to kiss her, but it didn't happen.

In fact, it never did. Melanie would have my heart for much of the next nine years but not one time did we ever kiss. I did, however, fantasize about her countless times over those years, and kissing didn't have a whole lot to do with what I was thinking about. I would think of her helpless, tied up, and gagged. As time went on, and I began to look at more violent pornography, things got worse for Melanie in my fantasies. In my mind, she was often in all sorts of peril, including being abducted by others to be cooked and eaten. She became my favorite girl to beat off to. Her resisting made her even more attractive.

Though she would resist me romantically, we still talked almost every day, but I wanted more. Looking back on it, her resisting me coincided with my developing more intense bondage masturbatory scenarios. I was also discovering more detailed websites and more detailed scenarios where women would be taken against their will. Instead of just a picture of a woman in bondage, a whole story would be told about a woman being kidnapped and tied up while she tried to resist.

When it came to Melanie, it was never me doing the kidnapping in my fantasies. I'd picture some old redneck couple that would grab her, tie her up, and gag her. She had a really feisty, no nonsense personality, so I'd imagine her fighting ferociously, always to no avail of course. She never got away. There wouldn't be any violence in these scenes, that kind of thing didn't turn me on, but her being helpless and incapacitated sure as hell did.

When we hung out, and I was around her, I never thought of all of the fantasies I had about her, it was just when I was alone, doing my thing, that they came into my mind. I respected her and I never forced myself on her. I always told myself that eventually she'd come around. Since I remained stubborn about wanting to be more than friends, we had a bit of a tumultuous relationship. We would argue, then meet a few days later in Manhattan and reconcile. Now it is hard not to feel that, at times, she strung me along, but back then I really thought that I loved her, and I was willing to be patient for it to work out. I was just head over heels for her. Despite the frequent ups and downs, we remained close over the years and relied on each other as go-to people when we were facing difficult moments in our lives. Unfortunately, the last time I saw her was up on the stand as a government witness during the trial. She was one of my alleged "victims."

My time at Molloy ended in 2002, when our baseball team won the city championship at Shea Stadium, the former home of the New York Mets. That was the last organized baseball game I ever played. I was a pretty good player, but was realistic about my ability, and although I could have played in college, I knew I didn't have pro potential, so I chose to focus more on the academic side of things.

I wanted to go to the University of Maryland the moment I saw the campus in February of 2002. The campus was big and absolutely gorgeous. It was away from home but close enough so that if I had to go home for a weekend it would not be a problem.

My dorm room freshman year was a quad, so I lived with three roommates all from Maryland. Two of them were personable, the other was unusually quiet but nonetheless a very nice kid. He was known as the "Rain Man" but eventually that changed to the "Reign Man" for reasons that I will explain later. One of them had a girlfriend who pretty much lived with us too, and she would tidy up the place, which was nice. The room was absolutely enormous and I'm proud to say that it was a major hub for parties.

With three roommates and all of the socializing going on, it was difficult, if not impossible, to surf the Internet for porn, so that part of my life was pushed into the background. Of course, I still had the same sort of fantasies, I was just engaging in them much less.

The vast majority of the girls at Maryland were gorgeous. It was difficult to focus in class sometimes, especially during the warm weather months. As hot as they were, I would always keep my real life and fantasy life separate. I would not sit in class and daydream about how I wish I could be hogtying and gagging every good looking woman in the room. Later on, when I discovered cannibalism-related porn, I didn't go around looking at beautiful women, while secretly imagining them trussed up like a turkey or roasting on a rotisserie. I have always been able to think about sex in a conventional way during the day. The weird stuff took over when I was alone on the computer.

There was one girl I met who I had a romantic interest in. Her name was Kate. She was from Maryland, short, petite, and had the cutest accent. We started to hang out and do things together; we usually ate together and spent a lot of time just talking in her room. She was attractive, but not a supermodel. She was the typical girl next door, which usually was the type that really got me going, and she knew a hell of a lot about football, which was amazing to me.

Though I had a romantic interest in her, we never hooked up. The stars never really aligned. Not only that but she had been seeing a guy who was thirty years old. To me, that was just crazy. Some of my close friends implored me to make a move so that I could "rescue her" from the "old" man, but I never did. A few times a week I would go to late night dining with her and one of her friends, and the two of them would just talk about this other guy. Sometimes I would get so incredibly pissed off by this, especially considering the fact that word had gotten around that I had a crush on her. I came close to exploding one night but I bit my tongue and never brought it up.

My confidence had been shot by the Melanie situation. Even though I was away in college, and she was still at Molloy, we talked almost every day through instant messaging. I still thought about her a lot. Since I had already invested so much time, energy, and love into Melanie, it was hard for me to let go and pursue another potential relationship.

Kate and the "old" man ended up breaking up but at that point I was just friends with her. We kept in contact after graduation. She stayed in Maryland and I went back to New York, but every time I visited Maryland we made plans to see each other and catch up. I could always count on getting together with her when I was in town. Even a couple of years after graduation some of our mutual friends still talked about the possibility of Kate and I hooking up and ending up together. Since I was still single and finally letting go of Melanie, I had seriously considered the possibility. Every two weeks I would get three days off, maybe I could go down and hang out with her. She had a job in the media; maybe she could come up to the media capital of the world? Most of my friends thought it should happen. I came very close to approaching her with the idea, and I swore that next time I was in town I would, but by then I had created a profile on OKCupid and I had just received the first message from the woman who would end up being my wife. So Kate and I never got serious.

As I got into my junior year, I decided to declare criminal justice as a second major. Some of the teachers I had were retired cops in Maryland and they made policing sound very interesting. I began to think about a career in law enforcement. It was nothing set in stone, but it was something that was at least an option. During the summer following my sophomore year, I had a well-paid internship in a corporate setting in Manhattan. It was a good experience, but there was no way I was going to sit in a cubicle in front of a computer until I was sixty-five years old. Offices were out of the question.

For the most part, I had the typical college experience. The four years went by way too fast. I made a lot of friends, went to a lot of parties, played pranks, got way too drunk too many times, and hooked up with girls.

When I say "hooked up" it means a lot of making out and messing around, but I never had sex in college. It was just something that was not on the top of my list of things that had to happen. I knew it would happen eventually, when the moment was right with the right person. I wasn't this sex crazed teenager who thought that it was mandatory that I lose my virginity in college. I was terrified about getting some random girl pregnant. I wanted to do well in school and have options and opportunities to have a successful life. Being a father at nineteen would have put the kibosh on that.

During the fall semester of my junior year, I was living with the quiet kid I had lived with in the quad during freshman year, the Rain Man. On one Friday afternoon, he had already left to go home for the weekend and I was having a serious computer issue. One of the computer tech guys on campus told me that I had to find a floppy disk, for God knows what reason, and I didn't have one. I called the Rain Man and he said that he had some in his closet. I thanked him, and he said "you're welcome" in the calmest, most nonchalant voice, which ended up surprising me considering what I soon discovered he had in plain view on his closet floor.

About a half second after opening his closet door, I completely forgot about the floppy disk. On his closet floor was easily the best porn DVD library on campus, possibly in the entire state of Maryland. I grabbed one of my duffel bags and loaded it up with forty something DVDs, called up one of my friends and told him I was coming over. Showing up a bit tired after lugging that bag across campus, everyone was amazed at what was inside. We laid a blanket out on the floor and organized the DVDs into even rows and columns. One of the guys took a picture and then we popped a video in.

We sampled quite a bit of his collection. One of the videos was titled "Black Reign," which is why he went from the Rain Man to the Reign Man. It was an odd collection for sure, with a lot of unconventional stuff. One that I still remember clearly was called "Bella Loves Jenna." It was a porno starring Jenna Jameson, about a woman being executed in the electric chair and then ending up in hell, where she was fucked six ways to Sunday by creepy looking demons. In almost every scene, there was this one midget demon that would show up on a tricycle and watch. It was mind-blowing how weird it was.

The Reign Man found out what had happened, but he didn't care. He almost seemed proud of it. He had absolutely no shame, and I should have taken that as a lesson at the time. As for me, the collection of weird, unconventional porn piqued my curiosity and got me searching on the Internet for stuff that might involve more obscure fetishes.

I don't remember what I first searched for, but it all led me to a website called Muki's Kitchen, which was a fetish site that was based around cannibalism. That was my first taste of cannibalism-related pornography. There were tons of gorgeous models on that website, depicted as food, ready to be served, but in a fun, sexy kind of way. Just like any type of porn, there is hardcore and there is softcore, and the presentation on this site was definitely on the mellower side of things. There was no blood or gore, just naked women who were typically laid out on a platter surrounded by vegetables with an apple in their mouth. There were photos of naked women being basted, and women being put on spits. I was totally turned on by these images. The website had a section titled "Related Links," so I clicked on that and found other websites that catered to cannibal porn. One was called the "Dolcett Girls Forum." It was a message board where users shared pictures and wrote fictional stories. Some of these were gory and involved fantasies of kidnapping and cooking non-consensual victims. One user's catchphrase was: "It's as easy as ABC: Abduction, Bondage, Cannibalism."

Muki's Kitchen was updated with new pictures once a week and the forum was updated multiple times a day with new pictures and stories. So, just like when I discovered the bondage and S & M stuff in the past, I would now imagine girls that I knew in the Muki's Kitchen photos and the kidnapping and cooking-related stories from the forum. The scenario I imagined in my mind while masturbating would always stop before the actual cooking. My fantasies never involved women actually dying or being eaten. It was all about the bondage, helplessness, and their lack of control. I am not saying this to make myself seem a certain way; it is just that the whole fetish world is a lot larger than people with vanilla tastes know. If one is into BDSM kind of stuff, there are literally about a thousand different spots they might be on the scale. It could go everywhere from someone being into verbal humiliation to someone who gets turned on by getting hung by their nipples from hooks.

When I was fantasizing, I would think about girls I knew, being abducted by others, tied up and gagged with the knowledge that they were going to be cooked and eaten for dinner, but the scene would never actually get there. When I discovered these sites, I didn't waste any time worrying about whether or not there was anything wrong with me. I had a large circle of friends and I was doing well in school. I was keeping everything fetish-related to myself and I intended to continue to do so.

The Dolcett Girls Forum had some more cannibal related pictures but they were cartoonish and kind of lame, but there were people on the forums that wrote some good stories about non-consensual victims. So I had the visual stimulation from Muki's Kitchen, and the written stories that would pique my interest and give me new things to think about. The same scene with different girls was fine, but it was kind of stale.

Meanwhile, college was just about over, and I needed to think of what I was going to do next. In the middle of senior year in college, I surprised everyone in my family by coming up to New York for the weekend to take the NYPD exam. I told them it was just an option, but I knew in my heart I was serious about it. I was going to become one of "New York's Finest".

2.

I scored a 99% on the NYPD entrance exam. I took it in October of 2005, while I was still in college. While that might sound impressive, but the only thing I was confused about was how in the hell I didn't get 100%. The test was an absolute joke. The hardest part of the exam was making sure I didn't drop my pencils on the floor. The majority of the questions went something like this:

> Officers Riley and Johnson responded to a burglary call on November 1 at 1910 hours. The burglary took place in a home located at 123 Anytime Lane. They were unable to ascertain a detailed description of the suspect(s) so they took the complaint report and made the proper notifications.
>
> Please answer the following based on the above information:
>
> What was the address of the reported burglary?

Seriously? This wasn't even a memory situation. All I had to do was look up at the short paragraph and find the answer. This was reading comprehension on the level of pre-school.

I was back in New York living with my father after graduation and was leaning heavily towards joining the NYPD. My family was supportive but their thought process was something like: All of that money for a college education and you want to be a police officer? I had done a lot of research on the department and found that there were plenty of opportunities to join specialized units and earn promotions. The benefits were outstanding too. I had the educational background needed with my bachelor's degrees to work my way up the ranks and become a supervisor. That was my long-term plan. I was not going to be a patrol officer my entire career. When I explained this to them, it made more sense but they still wished I would venture into something less dangerous.

I put together the avalanche of paperwork that I needed for the Applicant Processing Division. Next up was the psychological evaluation. They administered a 1,600 question multiple-choice exam with questions about everything under the sun. There were questions about racial biases, views on violence, finances, relationships, and whether or not I currently wet my bed. I answered everything honestly and ended up passing with no red flags popping up. A week later I had a face-to-face evaluation with an NYPD psychologist. We talked for about 30 minutes.

Of course, it never occurred to me to volunteer my unusual pornographic interests. It had never been an issue with how I lived my life or how I treated people, so I never brought it up. We touched on my upbringing, relationships with family and friends, my education, and my lifestyle while in college. I admitted to trying marijuana on three separate occasions while in college, but I was not worried that it would be an issue, and it wasn't.

Overall, I coasted through the academy. Much like the entrance exam, the academics were a total farce. Don't get me wrong, a lot of the material was absolutely critical for police officers to know. In order to graduate, you had to pass the final exam. The final exam was an open book test, for which the day before they spent half of the day teaching us how to utilize an index and a table of contents. So, there was no need to memorize and really understand when, and under what circumstances, you can legally stop someone, what constitutes "probable cause," or any other legal situation that a police officer needs to know before he or she hits the streets. In other words, if you really had no idea whether or not you could legally arrest someone in the situation that was given on the exam, no big deal. You could just look it up.

Once or twice during the week, if I wasn't too tired, I would check out some computer porn in the privacy of my bedroom. My brother was away in college so that made masturbating a lot more easy to accomplish. I was still down with the bondage and cannibal related pornography. My thing continued to be looking at pictures, reading stories, and imagining the women I knew in those dangerous and helpless situations. Around this time, I started using Facebook, so I often would seek out pictures of women I knew in sexy clothes or bikinis as a visual aid in my imaginary scenarios. For example, I would use a woman I knew dressed in a particular outfit in my fantasy where she would be abducted and tied up.

In December 2006, the police academy days were dwindling to a precious few. True to form, I passed everything easily and coasted under the radar. We were issued our service weapons and our shields. During one of the last afternoons, the precinct assignment sheets came in and our company sergeant began reading down the list. Since my last name begins with a "V," I had a while to wait to find out where I was going to be sent. Everyone before me who lived in Queens was given a Queens precinct, which I thought was great. I was familiar with Queens so that would be a great situation for me. Then it was my turn: "Valle. Three-Two."

The Three-Two was the 32nd Precinct. I didn't know anything

about it, but someone from another company asked me where I was assigned. When I told him the three-two, he winced and told me he was sorry. When I got home, I did some research. The three-two was right smack in the middle of Harlem, in the middle of one of the more violent precincts in all of New York City. I quickly learned one of the famous NYPD clichés: "It is what it is."

A big part of the reason that I was assigned to that precinct was because of Operation Impact, which was a program that Commissioner Raymond Kelly started. The idea was that the police department would flood the violent precincts with new rookies right out of the academy and put them on foot posts at nearly every corner. They would be there for six months until new rookies replaced them. The old rookies would either remain in the current precinct or be reassigned to another precinct within the borough.

Operation Impact made a whole lot of sense on the surface. A pair of cops on every street corner would deter drug dealing out in the open as well as violence out in the streets. The everyday citizen would feel safe. But simply deterring crime by being a presence was not good enough for the job. I soon found out that the department was a numbers beast with an insatiable appetite that needed constant feeding.

My first day at the precinct was all about orientation. An intimidating lieutenant lectured us about chain of command, and kept on nailing home the point that we were assigned to a very violent precinct, we needed to stay aware, and we had better be sharp. He went over the amount of homicides over the past twelve months and the number of guns that are typically recovered from the streets on a monthly basis. All of that was nice, but it wasn't until I went to lunch that I realized I needed to grow up quickly.

At lunchtime, I walked with a couple of other guys around the corner to get some food at some hole-in-the-wall Chinese place. There was bulletproof glass at the counter, and a locked gate that served as a barrier to the kitchen. I had never seen anything like this before. On the way back to the precinct, a police officer alerted us over the radio to a foot pursuit involving a man with a gun. The three of us rookies dropped our food and tried to figure out what the heck was going on. I tried to listen to the radio but the cop was yelling and I couldn't tell which way was up. There were police cars with screaming sirens zooming all over the place. They caught the guy like they usually do, but damn, what the hell was I getting in to?

We settled back into our orientation and that same lieutenant came in and said, "Now you all know I wasn't bullshitting you." After that, we received our squad assignments and schedule. My shift was from 5:30 pm to 2:05 am. It didn't take a genius to know that those hours are when most of the crime happens. The days off rotated; I would work five days, then be off for two, work five more, and be off for three. I received my assignment for New Year's Eve. Through some kind of error in paperwork, I was assigned to a mobile unit that involved patrolling in a van with one sergeant and seven other cops. I was the only new jack who was assigned to that so I was damn lucky.

Just like at the police academy, I intended to fly under the radar and not make a name for myself. I sat in the back of the van and kept quiet the majority of the night, while the sergeant and seven other veteran cops bullshitted and took bets on where the first homicide of the year would take place, a tradition they did every year. They were nice enough to include me, and I participated, but there wasn't much else for me to talk about with them. Veteran cops typically do not talk to the new guys right away, and with good reason. They need to be felt out and vetted for trust. The ball in Times Square dropped while we were in the van a few blocks away, the area was cleared out within ninety minutes, and we headed back to the precinct for the end of our shift. My first New Year's was a piece of cake.

Since my graduation from the police academy was in December, I was fortunate in that I was able to ease into things at the 32nd Precinct, largely because of the cold weather. There were not as many people outside that time of year, which also meant there were not as many crimes. It allowed me to comfortably get a general feel of how things were done there. At almost every roll call we were instructed to clear the corners of groups congregating, issue criminal court summonses ("C" Summonses) for violations like drinking in public, pissing, or trespassing, and to perform stop and frisks, which were known as "250s". Nearly every roll call ended with a boss saying "Cs and 250s."

Things got pretty comical when it came to clearing people off of the corners. I moved them off of my corner, so they went a couple of blocks away and then the cops over there would clear them. It was the same routine almost every night. Most of the time these people weren't even doing anything wrong. Standing on a corner isn't a crime. A lot of these people were poor and didn't have much else to do other than meet up and bullshit all night. Since the bosses would give you crap if there was a group on your corner, they always had to be moved. I wasn't a rebel just yet, but it still sucked having to do it.

Stop and Frisk was a very controversial issue when I was a cop. African Americans were complaining that they were being targeted and harassed by police. Civil rights groups like the ACLU were getting involved. Blacks and Hispanics were stopped a lot more than Whites, but Blacks and Hispanics were also committing most of the crimes where I was assigned, because practically all of the residents in that area were Black and Hispanic, so it was a bit of a Catch-22. If there was a robbery committed, and the description of the suspect was a male black in his twenties wearing a black hoodie, we would go around looking for people fitting that description. The victim would then be brought to the location where the individual was stopped and he or she would say yes or no as to whether we had the right guy. If it wasn't the person who committed the robbery, we'd take his info and record it on a stop and frisk report. That makes sense, and there is nothing wrong with that at all.

What became frustrating at times was that if you didn't stop someone after the robbery, or assault, or whatever, some bosses seemed to think that you weren't doing your job. You had to go over the radio and say you had a person stopped so that you would get a job number to put on your Stop and Frisk report. Some cops felt pressure to stop just about anyone so they wouldn't get chewed out. I was working with an officer once, hen someone was robbed. There was a teenage kid who somewhat fit the description of the individual we were looking for, but he was in a deli waiting for a sandwich. He actually waved at us as we drove by. I was driving the patrol car and I knew that he wasn't our perp, but the guy I worked with that day went all commando and told me to stop the car. He ran into the deli and told the kid to "get his hands on the fucking wall". It was embarrassing for me, but I am sure it was even worse for that innocent kid who had merely stopped in a store to get a sandwich.

"Stop and Frisk" got out of control when it became part of the monthly quotas. You cannot quantify an appropriate number of stop and frisks. They are either there, or they aren't. There were days when an obtuse boss demanded a certain number of stop and frisks. If I didn't see anyone that warranted a legal, bonafide stop and frisk, and I didn't want to deal with that boss's nonsense at the end of the shift, I came in with reports saying that I stopped people named Mickey Mantle and Joe DiMaggio.

There were times at the end of the month when either my partner or I was short of the required amount of stop and frisks but we would not illegally "flake" anybody. There were other cops who had no problem doing that though, and that's when things became a big problem. People randomly walking down a street, or through a park, would be stopped. One night in my final year, a sergeant on the streets ordered me to stop and frisk a person who was just walking through a park, and I refused to do it. We went back and forth and things got heated, but a gun run job that was called in saved me from a possible suspension. We dropped the argument and I raced in the patrol car to the housing projects. The illegal stop and frisk was never brought up again.

Quotas do exist, and most of the time I didn't have a problem with it. The NYPD referred to them as 'performance goals" and they told the press that cops would not be punished for failing to meet these goals. That is completely false, but I did understand that the job needed a way to measure performance. It would have been a problem if there were no consequences for being a lazy "hairbag," as they are called, and not making arrests or writing summonses. And there were plenty of hairbags. In my precinct, every month they wanted twenty parking summonses, five traffic summonses, two criminal court summonses, and one arrest. In a typical month you would have anywhere from seventeen to twenty days of patrol, factoring in days off, court, and other assignments out of the precinct. You could trip and fall and land on these numbers easily. If you were on vacation for a week during the month, you would try and scale the numbers back a little bit so that you don't come off as a superstar, but there were goody go-getters who didn't care and they still met the numbers, even if they had a lot fewer days on patrol.

The only time I had a problem with these quotas was the end of the month. If a cop didn't have an arrest yet, one of two things would happen. He or she would take it upon his or herself to spend the entire day looking for any random arrest or a supervisor would go out and look for one and assign it to him or her. They looked for something easy like trespassing, or a marijuana possession. This put a strain on everyone, especially during the summer months. It could be a very busy day out there when we needed as many cars out as possible, but one patrol car might be out just looking for that one arrest and if they got it, they were done for the day because they still had to process it. Any other time of the month, the unfortunate soul who was stopped would likely just be given a summons or simply left alone. So this is where I had the problem with quotas. On the 5th day of the month, a person might have gotten a slap on the wrist, but on the 30th day, he'd be arrested for doing the same exact thing just so the cop could meet the quota. Not good.

There were guys in my impact class that were super heroes as well as those who were do-nothings. I fell somewhere in the middle, which is exactly where I wanted to be. Other cops and even some supervisors began to see that my paperwork was always squared away and that I exhibited common sense. People were already predicting that I was going to be a supervisor one day.

When all was said and done, the 32nd Precinct was not as bad as I thought it was going to be. I was permanently assigned to the 26th Precinct at the end of my rodeo with Operation Impact in August 2007. I said my goodbyes, shook a lot of hands, unpacked my locker, and headed to the place where I would work for the next six years until the day that it all came crashing down.

On the porn side of things, everything was the same, for the most part anyway. I still lived at home and my little brother was still in college, so I had the room to myself. I started to spend more money on video clips, not necessarily cannibalism-exclusive, but any good clip with an actress that was portrayed in extreme peril. I kept a mental list of favorite actresses, not because they were the prettiest, but they did the best job acting as non-consensual, unwilling victims in whatever plot they were involved in. I'd memorize my favorite scenes and then picture women I knew as those victims. There were daily updates on the Dolcett Girls Forum; which brought me new pictures and new stories that I used in my masturbatory scenarios.

Every once in a great while I would consider contributing and writing something on the site, but I would quickly dismiss it. I was a little paranoid about someone finding out somehow who I was. If that happened, how would that affect my status with my job? How embarrassing would it be? At this point, I still deemed it too risky. Not because of potential criminality, that thought never crossed my mind. Why would it? I wasn't doing anything illegal. I thought it was risky simply because I didn't want anyone to find out about this part of who I was.

Socially, I didn't have much going on at the time. I went out with police friends on occasion, but because of my work hours it would be around one in the morning by the time we got to where we were going, so not much ever happened. It was more about unwinding and hanging out with the guys.

One of my coworkers told me I should check out the dating site eHarmony. He said he met his wife on there. I always thought online dating was a little embarrassing, but once I knew someone who had his own success story, I decided to give it a shot. As it was, being a cop, it was tough to meet people, given my work schedule. My first two years on the street, Melanie was still in college and I had gotten to the point where I had kind of given up wasting my time and energy on her. I began realizing that I was missing out on other opportunities. When I say "kind of" that didn't mean I would not continue to think of her. I would still think about Kate from Maryland sometimes as well.

I created both an eHarmony account and an OK Cupid account at some point in early 2009. I went on around 5 or 6 dates with women I had met on eHarmony, but didn't hit on anything that really felt right. Three of the dates I went on were painful; there was no chemistry at all, for either of us. There was one girl I went out with that I kind of liked who lived close to where I worked. Sometimes during work I'd drive to her building, she would come down and we would talk for a few minutes. She said she liked seeing me in uniform, so it scored some easy points for me. Then suddenly, she just stopped texting me. I tried calling and left a message, but I never heard back.

There was another girl, who I really liked, who lived on Long Island and was a teacher. We both still lived at home so it was hard to really spend time together. We had gone on three dates and it seemed that we really hit it off. We began talking about booking a hotel room and getting more intimate.

Then, one day out of the blue, she texted me that she really liked me but she didn't think she could be in a serious relationship with a cop. That one hurt, because I really liked her. I got that message in the middle of a serious job at work. Someone had gotten shot, and I was at the crime scene trying to interview witnesses when the phone buzzed and I got the message that she didn't want to be with me because of my job. At that point, I didn't even bother to try and sell myself to her.

It was important for me to find a woman that was okay with what I did for work. I was proud of being a cop, and I was proud to tell people that I worked for the NYPD. If a woman wasn't okay with that, I understood. I just wished they would tell me from the get-go instead of wasting my time, as well as their own. In all fairness, maybe you don't always know these things until you get involved.

There were some really crappy days when I worked as a police officer. I saw a lot of crazy stuff, and there were times when the stress was unreal. I had to make the right decision every single time or there would be serious consequences, especially in a community where a lot of people hated cops. My golden rule was to never take a previous incident that may have pissed me off into the next job. The next call might involve someone who really needed help, which is what I enjoyed the most about being a police officer, helping people who really needed help. I also tried to never take the job home with me. For the most part, I was really good at compartmentalizing; call to call, day to day, cop and civilian, and clearly, fantasy and reality.

Despite anything I encountered on the streets, what frustrated me the most about police work was the internal departmental stuff. In addition to the stop and frisk and quota issues, the Chief of Patrol would pick a random Tuesday and make it cell phone initiative day for example. This meant that every cop had to come in with two cell phone tickets, which meant busting people who were driving while talking on the phone. Every hour, we had to call the precinct and report our progress. They were easy violations to get and most of the time I got them, but it was the idea of being babysat, and having supervisors breathing down our necks, when there is a lot of other stuff to do, that irked me. The time my partner and I spent sitting in one spot for two hours, looking for people driving while talking on their cell phone, meant that the rest of our sector was not being patrolled. It royally ticked me off if someone got robbed or assaulted while I was just sitting in my cruiser because the lieutenant wanted a cell phone summons that could easily come at any time during the month.

Another night in the middle of one summer, a lieutenant called each patrol car to a major intersection outside of one of the housing projects. He stood out there like a maniac and pointed out people, all African-American, who were jaywalking, and ordered the cops to issue "C" summonses to them. It was a lawful order, so there was nothing we could do. If we disobeyed he could suspend us. Eventually, it was my turn, and my hands were tied. There I was, an NYPD cop, writing summonses to people from the housing projects who were jaywalking, something most people, including me, do every single day. I never felt lower as a cop than that night when I wrote my summonses. I had friends who worked in more affluent areas of Manhattan, and I had never heard of any jaywalking enforcement initiatives on the prosperous Upper East Side.

As I said before, the NYPD is obsessed with numbers. That didn't just apply to summonses and arrests. It also applied to crime numbers for the precincts. One afternoon, someone fired a gun from one street corner. That corner was within the confines of the 30th Precinct. The bullet struck someone across the street. The guy who got hit was within our precinct. So we set up a crime scene, the guy who got shot was removed to the hospital, and for thirty minutes bosses from each precinct argued with each other about who was going to be hit with the felony assault number. Cops from both precincts who would be manning the crime scene waited until it was finally decided that it was ours.

I was able to handle anything on the outside, the shootings, the stabbings, the deaths, everything, by treating it almost like I was in a movie. That was my way of coping with it. But it was the internal stuff – the harassment for numbers, the dumb initiatives, questionable orders from bosses - that frustrated me to no end.

I drew my gun plenty of times, but never fired it. The closest I ever came was in 2007, my first year on the street, during a vehicle checkpoint. Some guy just blew right through it. I was standing right in the middle of the street and he was gunning right for me. I pulled the gun out and almost fired, but there were a lot of people around and I ran the risk of hitting someone if I missed. I saw a lot of people out of the corner of my eye ducking. Instead, I quickly got out of the way, ran towards my car, and tried to follow in pursuit, but he was already long gone. It sucked that he got away, but I knew I had made the right call by not shooting.

I started to become a bit of a rebel. There was a period when the Internal Affairs Bureau was in traffic court monitoring cops' testimonies. They were looking to take vacation days away from cops for not having accurate notes. My way of staying away from this was to stop writing tickets that had a chance of winding up in traffic court. I still met my quotas, but I began writing tickets that could be prepaid instead of requiring a court appearance. If I was somehow called to traffic court, which wasn't often, I took advantage of the NYPD's unlimited sick leave policy and called out sick. My absence meant that the ticket was dismissed, but I couldn't care less about my record in traffic court. Calling out sick was my way of protesting Internal Affairs. Every cop complained about going to traffic court and possibly losing vacation days if they lost and their notes weren't perfect, but no one else on my shift had the balls to do what I did. Nearly everyone on the midnight shift would call out sick for traffic court though, so it was nice to see that unity among the troops.

People seemingly thought of me as the leader of our squad, and would call me with questions even before they called the sergeants. Men and women that I worked with told me that whatever squad ends up with me as their supervisor would be damn lucky. I wasn't the kind of guy who was a company man or who drank the "Kool-Aid" and I knew I would always stay that way. In all my time on the streets, I never received a civilian complaint. The greatest compliment I received was from a sergeant, who told my partner and me that when we were responding to a job, he never had to worry that we were going to screw things up.

I was never shot at, and no one ever charged me with a knife or any other deadly weapon. I did get hurt twice though. The first time was in 2009 while driving with the lights and sirens on to an emergency. As I was zipping through traffic heading northbound, someone going east ran a red light and I T-boned him going about fifty m.p.h. Neither my partner nor I was wearing our seatbelts, but we were relatively okay. The airbag did most of the damage on me, ripping off a lot of skin from my left forearm. There was a lot of blood and I have a permanent scar. The other driver and his passenger were also okay, thank God.

It might alarm people that I, a police officer, was not wearing my seatbelt. "Click it or ticket" is a popular saying. Most of the people I worked with didn't wear seatbelts, and I seldom wore mine while I was on duty. The NYPD Patrol Guide lists wearing seatbelts as a requirement, and failure to do so could cost vacation days, but there is a simple reason why most of us didn't wear them. There were times when arriving at an emergency, I had to exit the vehicle as quickly as possible. If I was wearing the seatbelt, there was a chance that it could get caught on my gun belt and that would prevent me from immediately getting out of the car to provide help to whoever needed it. Seconds mattered during emergencies.

The second time I was injured was during my last year on patrol in 2012. Three other cops and I were trying to bring down an absolute beast of a man who was high on PCP, which seemed to give him superhuman strength. A sergeant showed up and sprayed her mace to try and incapacitate him, but it ended up going squarely in my eyes. She couldn't have hit me any better if she was actually aiming for me. An hour later, we were able to laugh about it, but it wasn't funny at all while tears and snot were flying out of me after she sprayed me.

As far as being a "cop" forever, my plan was to work my way up the ranks as high as the job would let me go. I passed the sergeant's exam on my first attempt, and I was about a month away from being promoted before everything came crashing down.

3.

In 2009, I had three years in with the NYPD and I was still living at home with my father. One night when I was surfing the web I came across something called the Dark Fetish Network through one of those "related sites" kind of links on another BDSM porn site I was looking at. . I liked the site and I started spending more and more time there.

I would usually log on to DFN after I got home from work around one in the morning. I had a little routine. I would check my e-mail and Facebook, maybe take a look at the box score of the Yankees game, and then I would hit DFN.

DFN was sort of like a social media site for people with unusual sexual fantasies. It covered the whole spectrum as far as fetishes go. There was bondage, cannibalism, vore, torture, castration, pissing, feces, slavery, leather, executions, mummification; it just went on and on. Most of the stuff did not appeal to me, but it was obvious there was something there for everyone with an unusual sexual fetish, and clearly, I was one of those people.

The intro to DFN said it all. "Welcome to the social network where you won't feel like an outcast cause of your 'dark' fetish. Why? Because this place is created by people like you, FOR people like you! So feel free to look around, meet some crazy (in a good way!) people and become part of our growing ADULTS ONLY (18+) community. Please also remember that THIS PLACE IS ABOUT FANTASIES ONLY, so play safe!"

I got even more into the site when I started browsing through photo albums and saw that some members posted pictures of women that they said they knew. They looked like photos that had been pulled from Facebook pages. The theme around all of these photos was "What Would You do With Her?" and people left comments that were tailored to their personal sexual fetishes on the photos of the women. If you were into sleep stuff, then maybe you would say you wanted to chloroform her and play with her body, if you were into BDSM, you might say that you would hogtie her and force her to submit to you. This whole thing drew me in pretty much right away.

I decided to create an account and check it out. I created a profile with the user name "Girlmeat Hunter" and wrote that I was interested in fantasies involving kidnapping, bondage, and cannibalism. My thing was that my fantasies and scenarios all involved non-consensual victims. Others enjoyed fantasies involving women who would consent to being tortured, hung, eaten, or whatever. The consensual scenarios didn't appeal to me in my own fantasies. It wasn't like I was turned on by a woman that wanted to be kidnapped, that ruined the whole thing.

I noticed that the website hammered home the fact that this was all fantasy only, so I echoed that in my profile just to be safe. I knew of course that I would never hurt anyone, despite mentally enjoying graphic, brutal scenarios involving women that I knew, but I thought it was good to put that disclaimer in my profile just to be sure. This is the crux of the whole thing really. They are called fantasies for a reason, at least to most of us who have such odd fantasies, myself included. This was a site for people to openly express their fetishes, not to plan crimes.

Before long, I had created my very own "What Would You Do?" album. I uploaded Facebook pictures of about ten women I knew and I posted them in the album. I didn't use names at this point, it was just "Girl #1, Girl #2," and so on. I remember when I did this because it was early on a Friday morning, and I was going to travel down to Maryland for a football game at the university for the weekend. When I was finished posting the pictures, I packed up and left for Maryland.

When I came back Sunday night, I logged back in to DFN and saw that I had around 50 comments from other users about the photos that I had put up. All sorts of people had commented on them, talking of ideas and scenarios around what they would do with the women that I posted. Most of them were bondage and cannibal related comments. I came to realize that was kind of the unofficial rule of the site; you would read the user's profile and leave comments related to that person's sexual fetishes, it was sort of just how it was done.

I read all of the comments posted in response to the photos of each of the ten or so women I posted and thought about how interesting and detailed some of them were. I ended up thinking about some of them later when I beat off, incorporating the ones that I liked best into the scenarios that I thought of. Little did I know that this was the beginning of a nightmare.

Nevertheless, life had settled into a routine. I was still living at home, I worked a lot, I went on dates, and to satisfy myself sexually, I went on DFN.

Then I met the woman who became my wife.

4.

Her name was Kathleen. We met on OKCupid. She was the first and only woman I met on that dating site. I sent the first message. I had in my profile that I worked as a police officer. I remember this because when she replied she said she thought me being a cop was so cool. She said that she grew up in a family out west where her father was a cop and that she understood the crazy hours and unpredictability of the schedule.

That earned major points with me right away because other girls I tried to date didn't want any part of that schedule, or the fact that I was a cop. Since I had a schedule with rotating days off, there were long periods where I would work on weekends and have days off during the week. Kathleen understood this, so that hurdle was already cleared.

We exchanged maybe three or four messages, and things were going smoothly so we agreed to meet. I told my partner at work about it and I asked him to recommend a good place for a first date. He told me about a place called Bistro 1018. He said it was a good spot to take a woman, so I set it up with Kathleen. We decided to meet on a Saturday night which was the same night as a Yankees playoff game in October. You know I like a woman if I miss a Yankees playoff game to take her out, because that's a big deal!

The 10th of October, 2009, was a pretty cold night and I left for our first date wearing a black turtleneck, jeans, and a black leather jacket. The plan was to meet at eight p.m. She lived in Harlem, which was probably about a thirty minute bus ride away. I didn't offer to pick her up because it was an online dating thing, and I figured she would feel safer with the whole scene if we just met at the restaurant. She said it was an easy bus ride and she'd be there around a quarter to eight.

I got there around 7:40 and I waited outside on the corner. It was windy and cold. 7:45, 7:50, 7:55, I kept checking my phone every few minutes and nothing. 8:00, 8:05, 8:10, still nothing. I was freezing my ass off. I also was wondering if she was okay, or if maybe she had stood me up. Finally, I texted her, asking if everything was all right and I told her that I was waiting outside.

About a minute later, I got a reply and her text said she was already inside. I turned around, looked at the front door and there she was, looking at me and beaming with laughter. I loved her smile and the way she kind of tilted her head back when she laughed. This little silly moment was a great icebreaker for our first date.

Dinner was fantastic. I had chicken and pasta and she had lobster bisque. Things were going well and it was obvious that we had some chemistry. We kept making a lot of eye contact and there was a lot of laughter. I didn't want the night to end, so I asked her if she wanted to go catch a movie. She said yes, and before we left, we shared Crème Brûlée for dessert. When we got outside it was cold, and she wasn't dressed very warmly, so I put my jacket over her shoulders while we walked to my car.

We saw *Couples Retreat* with Vince Vaughn. During the movie, I put my arm around her and she nestled into my chest. I remember thinking, "Holy shit, it might happen tonight." I was so excited just thinking about what might go down later, that I was not paying attention to the movie at all, not even a little bit. I remember her being close to me, the smell of her perfume, our bodies touching. I was getting more and more turned on as the movie progressed.

When the movie ended, we held hands as we walked back to the car. Her place was about a 20-25 minute ride away, which was more than enough time to either seal the deal or totally screw the whole thing up. I was excited and a little nervous. I have no idea what we talked about during the drive back. I decided that I would let her make the call as to what was going to happen later. The night was great but I didn't want to push and ruin everything. The most I would do is kiss her good night, and if she wanted to invite me upstairs, of course, I wouldn't turn it down.

I parked right in front of her place, and she leaned in and gave me a really passionate kiss. It was amazing. It was that kind of kiss that lets you know that it won't be the last one. She thanked me for a great night and said, "Text me." Then she got out of the car. I stayed there watching, waiting until she safely got in her building, then I left.

I wasn't at all disappointed that things didn't continue that night. I was on a cloud during my whole drive home. She was gorgeous, we had such a great time, and we really clicked. She was smart, funny, and seemed like a really great person who would be a lot of fun to be around.

When I got home, I washed up, and got into bed. I thought about the night, thought about her and I started getting a hard on. I jerked off, imagining her being chloroformed and kidnapped by a crazy couple, stripped naked, and laid out on a platter with an apple in her mouth. She was the newest addition to my scenarios.

We hung out again the following weekend on Sunday night, going to dinner and a comedy club. When we left, she gave me a passionate kiss right out in the street. Later, I drove her home and again wondered if tonight was going to be the night. That is the thing about still being a virgin at 25 years of age, at some point it becomes less about the sex, and more about just getting it over with so you don't have to think about it anymore.

I suggested that we go to a private, quiet area that I knew about and we could hang out for a bit. This was to give the hint that I wanted things to progress and mess around with her for a bit but I didn't want to push myself into her place. She told me that it wasn't a good night for that, as it was really late and she had to get up early for work. I got all childlike and even started to beg a little. She laughed and said that she was very sorry but it was really just because of work.

Again, I was cool with that. I wanted to have sex, both because I found her ridiculously attractive, and because I wanted to get that monkey off my back once and for all. But still we had a lot of fun and I could not imagine us not seeing each other again, so I was satisfied.

We stayed in touch flirting and texting a lot. One Saturday night, I was in the patrol car with my partner just chilling, listening to the Yankees game and Kathleen texted me and asked how my night was going. I asked her what she was up to. She said that she was going to go to a party that night but she blew it off. She said something like; "I thought it would be a lot more fun if you came over after work, so we can watch *Arrested Development.* I have cranberry juice and cheap vodka." While I still had never had sex, I had been around enough to know what this meant.

I showed my partner the text message. I was psyched. He was driving the car that night. I told him to park the car on a quiet street and stay there so we didn't run into some issue that would cause me to stay late. If we ran into an arrest, somehow he was going to take it. He laughed and of course he agreed. We chilled the rest of the night.

I always had a set of clothes in my work locker in case I wanted to go out when I got off patrol. I changed clothes and went to her place excited as hell. I rang the buzzer and she came down and let me in. She was wearing a white tank top, pajama pants, and flip-flops. She looked so cute. I was a little nervous, but more excited than anything.

She poured some drinks and we started watching *Arrested Development*. We watched maybe three or four episodes, and then I started to climb all over her. She was into it and we started making out like a couple of wild animals.

This still wasn't the night though. When you have waited as long as I had, you sort of expect the act itself to be treated with a sort of reverence; I could wait a little longer, if she needed me to.

I did spend the night though. I slept in bed with her and we cuddled until the morning. She had the cutest little snore. Though we still hadn't done it, and I felt like I was going to explode, things still felt okay. I lay next to her with my arm around her and I was happy. I hadn't slept much that night. I just listened to her snore and looked at her. I remember thinking that there really might be something special with this girl.

The next morning we woke up and got coffee at Starbucks, and then I drove her to church. She liked to go to church on Sundays. She kissed me again, and I left. Between that day, and the next time I saw her, she had been abducted and tied up a few more times, in my mind.

The following Saturday night we texted each other and she told me to come over. She wanted to order pizza and watch a movie. After work, I went to a liquor store and bought the most expensive bottle of wine I could find, which in Harlem was not saying a whole lot. I went over to her place with one thing in mind. Tonight was going to be the night.

I got to her place, poured two glasses of wine, and we put a movie on. I have no idea what we were watching. The pizza came and we ate a little bit. Maybe thirty minutes or an hour later, we both had a nice buzz going and I pounced on her. It was like all of my years of waiting came out all at once.

We started out on the couch; I kissed her, and licked and lightly bit her neck. She let out a crazy moan. She stood up and led me by the hand and we literally ran into the bedroom

It was amazing. Better than I ever imagined it.

Things went quickly after that. Maybe a week or two after we had sex for the first time, we made it official that we were a couple. She moved in to a small apartment on the Upper East Side with a friend of hers who was also a teacher. We had a pretty set routine. I would usually go to her place after work two or three times a week. When I did, she would stay up late and wait for me. Some nights we just talked about our days, some nights we talked and had sex. The sex was always great, and it really seemed like we got each other. I woke up with her early in the morning and drove her to work, and then I went back home to my dad's where I was still living. I was really falling for her. It felt like love.

I spent most of my days off with her. We went out a lot and hit different spots in NYC. She was from Nevada and she had only been in New York for a couple of years, so I played the local and showed her around. I started to introduce her to my friends and co-workers. When my work schedule permitted, I was able to join her for a few of those Friday teacher happy hours and I was meeting a lot of her friends. Other days, we just hung out at her place, watched TV or movies, and I cooked dinner for her and her roommate when she was around. Kathleen loved my tacos.

Of course throughout all of this, I was on the Dark Fetish Network. So was Kathleen. I started to put her pictures up on the site. I got a decent amount of cannibal-related comments about her, about the same amount as some of the photos of other women I had put on there before. She had become my favorite woman to fantasize about. It was easier to picture her in the scenarios because I knew what she looked like naked.

About a year after our first date, we moved in together. It was a small, overpriced Manhattan apartment with a lot of maintenance issues, but it was our first home. I got home from work around 12:15 am or so. She was in bed but always greeted me when I came home and asked if I was okay. I had fallen for her, and she was head over heels for me. One day we were out with some of her friends at a teacher happy hour, and she just turned to me and said, "Gil, I am so happy with you."

I started thinking about forever. Is she really the one? I didn't see a reason not to think so. I never felt as passionate about her as I did Melanie, the first girl who had my heart, but I did love Kathleen for sure. I knew that I wanted to be with her and protect her.

She had gone to college at Gonzaga University in Spokane, WA. They had a great basketball team that she followed rabidly. Their mascot was a bulldog. She always wanted one. If she was in the car with me while I was driving, and she spotted a bulldog being walked, she would yell "Bulldog, bulldog, bulldog!" and I had to pull over so she could pet it.

We ended up with our own bulldog puppy named Dudley. It was obvious that Dudley was the "trial child." She was feeling me out, wanting to see how I would take care of the dog.

A month later, on a random January day in 2011, we found out that she was pregnant. It was a total surprise. I was only 26 years old and she was 25. The first thing I said when I found out was "Kathleen, we can't do this!" Up to this point in my life, everything had been nice and mapped out. Everything was structured. She was freaking out too. We were both nervous about telling our parents. After we talked for a while, I calmed down and I started thinking about finances. We talked it through and once I knew that we would be able to do it financially, I welcomed the idea. Even if there was a problem with finances, we would have found a way. An abortion was 100% out of the question for both of us. It was going to happen. We were going to become parents.

All of my focus became about her and the baby. For all intents and purposes, we were married, but the wedding was still far down the road. I started concentrating on being the best parent I could be. I was working constantly on finding a place where we could start our family, and making sure that we had the baby's room fully furnished. I borrowed

$16,000 against my retirement to make sure we had the best of everything for the baby. I read books on parenting. Most of the reading I did was while I was at work during down time.

My partner was the first person I told. He thought it was absolutely great. We were nervous as hell to do this, but after three months, we both told our parents. We were surprised at how well everyone took it. We were both expecting our dads to freak out, but they were both so happy. I told her father that he didn't have to worry about Kathleen. I would always take care of her. He said he knew that, and he would never worry about her with me.

When she started to show, I drove her to work every single morning. I did not want her to have to deal with the bus and the subway. We found a new place, a spacious two bedroom apartment ten minutes from where I grew up in Queens. We used the money that I borrowed against my retirement to furnish the new apartment. Kathleen picked out a lot of the stuff that we needed for the baby's nursery.

I still was playing around on DFN. At this point in the game, I was pretty well-known on the site and I had about fifteen to twenty people I would chat with from time to time. These chats were never about the whole "How are you doing, how was your day?" thing, of course. No one knew who I really was or where I lived, and I didn't know that about them either. It was usually, "Hey, got some time to play around a bit?" Then we'd either continue an old story or just start a new one from the beginning.

I had a sergeant's test coming up in October, right around the time the baby was due to be born. I put in a ton of work studying for the test. It was a very challenging exam. I wanted to pass the test because it meant more money for my new family and me. Not only that, but I would also not be just a "cop" anymore. I would be one of the people in charge, and my summons writing days would be over.

Suddenly, one night in late September 2011, Kathleen's water broke. I was at the dog park with Dudley. It was actually Dudley's birthday and the usual group at the dog park was having a little party for him. Kathleen was resting at home, then texted me and told me the news. While I would like to say I remained calm, I immediately freaked out. This was a full two weeks early. I sprinted with Dudley back to the apartment. I was a sweaty mess and flipping out but she calmed me down right away. She told me that we had time, and that I should not worry, that I should relax. We had to pack an overnight bag, I had to bring Dudley to my mom's and so on. I calmed down a bit, but my mind was racing. I kissed her really quickly, asking if she was in pain, and if she was okay. She was really composed, cool, and collected, and told me again what I had to do. The first thing I did was bring Dudley to my mom's. On the way there, I called both of my parents. I am sure they could tell how nervous I was because they both told me to relax and that everything would be okay.

When I got back to the apartment, Kathleen had managed to pack a quick overnight bag for us. I was ready to go, but she said we still had plenty of time if I wanted to take a quick shower. I took a really quick five minute shower to cool down and freshen up, then I got dressed and we were ready to go.

It was a long, tough night once we got to the hospital. I think I was more nervous than Kathleen. Initially, she was refusing the epidural injection to ease some of her pain, but it reached a point where it was unbearable for her. The nurse who gave her the injection screwed it up somehow and it had no effect. In fact, she was in more pain. I was frantic and ran out into the hallway asking for a doctor or a nurse who knew what the hell they were doing.

Eventually, it all settled down, and at 6:22 in the morning I held my baby daughter for the first time. I had seen pictures of her on the ultrasounds and felt her kick when I would put my hand on Kathleen's stomach, but this was different. This was my baby. The joy I felt was overwhelming. She stopped crying when I held her, like she knew exactly who I was.

The first few days with the baby were exciting and hectic. I was able to take a week off from work. We had family and friends coming to congratulate us and see the baby. It actually was all like a big blur. We were a happy family. The baby was healthy; we were healthy, both mentally and physically.

As with most couples that have become parents, our sex life diminished a bit after the baby came. As good as our sex was, the thought never entered my mind to spice up our sex life with some kink. So like most married couples, our sex life started to slow down.

They would argue during the trial that our sex life diminished because I was too busy concocting plans to kidnap and eat women, but in reality, we had a newborn baby who drained a lot of our energy. Kathleen got up between six and seven when the baby woke up. I stayed in bed because I had to go to work, and I needed to make sure I got enough rest. Kathleen would put the baby down for a nap around nine-thirty or ten, and then come to bed exhausted. I was either up by that time, or I stayed in bed with her until the baby woke up. When the baby woke up, it was my turn to take care of her. Kathleen would often get up with me and breastfeed the baby, and then she would usually rest while I took care of her and played with her.

I passed the sergeant's exam two weeks after the baby was born. Kathleen's mom flew in from Nevada and stayed with us for two weeks so I could cram for the test and not have my attention divided, worrying about whether or not Kathleen had everything she needed with an infant. I was able to go to the library or to my mom's to study. Kathleen was one hundred percent behind me putting all of my effort into the exam. She knew how important it was to me, and to our future. I scored an 81/100 on the test, which is pretty much acing it, because average scores are low 70s. I was relieved and excited, and now that the exam was over, I could focus on being a father, and think more about the wedding.

Kathleen left her job and was a full-time stay at home mom. She wanted that, and we both thought that would be best for our daughter as well. Even though money was very tight for us at this point, I made enough money where I could take care of rent, my bills, her bills, and still have enough for an occasional luxury. Since she wasn't working anymore, she had no income so I gave her around $600 a month so that she could take care of her bills and still have enough to go out and enjoy herself from time to time. We were able to live quite comfortably within our means. With Kathleen staying home with the baby, I did most of the grocery shopping. If she needed some items, she made a list for me. I was doing what a man is supposed to do. I was providing for my family and I loved it.

Kathleen fully understood our financial situation. She had an engagement ring that belonged to her grandmother. She gave it to me and told me not to spend money on a ring. She told me to just give that to her when I am ready. I really appreciated this. Kathleen was not a material girl. Everything was for the baby, but still, we wanted to have our wedding. We wanted to celebrate our love and our family with our loved ones.

On Valentine's Day 2012, we went out to a very fancy Italian restaurant called Il Toscano in Queens. We both dressed up nicely, and I proposed to her there. I didn't get down on a knee and make a whole scene in front of everyone. I took the ring out of my pocket and proposed. I said to her that she already knows that I want to spend the rest of my life with her, but that we should make it official already. The smile on her face could light up a room. Her eyes were filled with tears. I slipped the ring on her finger; we held hands and just smiled at each other for what seemed like forever.

Our parents both helped out with the wedding costs. My dad gave me $5,000. We wanted a small wedding with just immediate family and a few friends. I wanted the wedding to be local, but she was dead set on getting married in Gonzaga.

I wanted to get married in New York. We met there, and our lives were there. We went back and forth a bit, but I caved and we finally settled on Spokane. It ended up being wonderful. I loved it out there and I wanted to go back. While she was in college, she babysat this really rich couple's children and she got really close with them. They stayed in touch over the years. They had a little house on their huge estate, and they let us stay there for the 10 days or so we were there.

Everyone from my immediate family was able to go, but not one of my work friends could make it. I knew they couldn't. It was too long of a trip and it was expensive. Plus, it was in June and it was tough at that time of the year to take time off from work. That was a little bit of a let down. She had a few friends from Reno there, but overall it was a very small wedding with only about twenty people in attendance. It was a lovely wedding though. We had our big wedding cake, but Kathleen also surprised me with a small cake of an NYPD Patrol Car. It was so cool and so perfectly done. On the side of the car where the precinct would ordinarily be marked, our wedding date was there instead.

Life at home continued as normal until one night I came home from work and went to let Dudley out of the crate to take him for a walk. Kathleen got out of bed and met me in the hallway, and said, "Dudley has to go." She was really angry, not crying or anything. We sat down in the kitchen and I asked her what happened. She said that when she was trying to put him in the crate around eight o'clock, he snapped at her and bit her hand. Dudley was sixteen months old and he was a bit destructive at times. He liked to play rough with me, but he had never done anything like that before. While we were talking, Dudley was whimpering in the crate wanting me to take him out to go to the bathroom. I looked at Kathleen's hand a few times while she was talking to me and it seemed to look okay, so I continued to try to convince her to change her mind, but she kept on bringing it back to the baby. "Go look at your sleeping daughter and tell me that you want to take a chance with this," she said to me. I had no ground to stand on. I loved this dog to death, but I couldn't argue against the possibility that he might hurt our daughter. Despite what had happened to Kathleen, I didn't think there was a chance in the world that Dudley would snap at our daughter. I tried to say that this was an isolated incident, but her mind was made up and she was right. She sternly said, "If you are going to leave it to me to find a home for him, fine."

I heard Dudley whimpering some more and I felt myself getting choked up. I didn't want to cry in front of her, so I held it in. She went back to bed, and then I started to lose it. I let him out of the crate, and he greeted me like he did every single night, like I was the best person on the planet. While he was jumping on me and playing, I was starting to cry a bit. I put his leash on, and then gained my composure before I took him for a walk. I called my mother and told her what happened, and that I needed her to take him ASAP. She, of course, said, "No problem." She loved that dog too. She was a ten minute drive away, so I put him in the car and drove him over. Then I went back home, packed all of his stuff and drove that over.

I went to bed and when I woke up the next morning, I sat in the kitchen by myself and looked over at where the crate used to be. Normally I'd be taking him for a walk and then feeding him, but there was nothing to do with the dog and I got choked up again. Kathleen came into the kitchen and asked me what had happened. I told her that I brought Dudley to my mom's. Kathleen told me that it's only temporary, and that when he is a little calmer we can take him back. She appreciated what I did and knew I was upset. On one of my days off every week, I picked him up and brought him over and he'd spend the day with us. The arrangement ended up not being so bad since my mom came through. On my days off, we'd do things as a family. Money was still tight, but on occasion we would go out to lunch. Most often we'd take the baby to the park or visit with my dad or mom so they could see the baby. This ended up becoming something that we would fight about. It never got to the point where we were yelling, but this was always something that hung over our heads. Kathleen said that I was spending too much time worrying about making sure my parents were happy. She said the only people I need to worry about making happy were her and our baby.

My parents never breathed down our necks at all. They both lived within ten minutes of us and it was easy for them to be a part of our lives. I had to strike a balance somehow. I wanted Kathleen and I to have our own lives with our baby, but I did not think that us going to visit my dad once a week, or him coming over for an hour once a week, was a big deal at all. To me, it was what families did, but she had a problem with it. She didn't really like my parents. Her parents had been married for thirty years, and mine were divorced and couldn't even be civil enough to have a conversation with each other. My father could be a bit condescending at times, but he was never disrespectful to Kathleen and he just melted around the baby. My mother would sometimes spew out whatever was on her mind. It was not always appropriate, and that made Kathleen uncomfortable at times, but she was very good with the baby.

The situation with Kathleen and my parents was not an easy thing to deal with, but they were who they were, and they weren't going to change. Sometimes, I made up excuses to my parents about why we couldn't see them. I would say the baby didn't sleep last night and that we're all too tired. It was pissing me off. Her mom would come and stay with us for two weeks straight, and I had no problem with friends of hers coming over whenever they wanted, but us spending an hour a week with my parents was a problem.

I tried to be patient with her about such things, as I knew that things were not always easy for her. She had told me once that while she was in college, she had gone through a period of time when she was depressed. Now, she seemed more than fine to me. We were happy, and we had a good life. We had the disagreement over the amount of time spent with my parents, but not much else other than that.

It never occurred to me to cheat on her, or anything like that. Melanie would sometimes creep into my mind and I'd wonder how things might have played out with her, but it wasn't very frequent. At one point, Melanie invited me to her new place. She said I could come after work for drinks, other times she said I should bring the wife and baby. I never went through with it because of the temptation that might lead to.

Despite the minor problems between Kathleen and me, being a father was amazing. I was so proud of being a dad. I loved talking about the baby to my cop friends, I am sure I drove a lot of them crazy. Even though she was just a baby, we had our own little thing going on. I had a short buzz cut at the time, so I would put her up on my shoulders and she loved to pat and rub my hair. Sometimes I'd trot with her on my shoulders and hum a cowboy song or something and she'd always laugh. When we would go in the car, as Kathleen was securing her in her car seat, she would sometimes cry when she first was put there, so I would go to the back window, make eye contact with the baby and start making silly faces. The crying would stop instantly, and she would start smiling and laughing. I loved my daughter and I loved being a dad. One morning, I was teaching her colors. I didn't notice Kathleen watching us, but when I looked up she was smiling. She said, "You know, I don't think I say this enough, but you're a really great dad." From time to time, she said things like that, or that she loved how silly I was with the baby, and it always made me feel good.

When Dudley was banished, the porn frequency picked up a bit. I have to admit I harbored a bit of ill will about the whole thing. I had my own little group of people I would talk to on DFN more often than others. I weeded out most of the people that didn't do my thing the way I liked to do it. Just like me, the people I role-played with in "my group" liked focusing on details. We didn't just rush through a scene and finish in an hour. Sometimes we would play it out over a couple of weeks, an hour or two whenever we were both online at the same time. It wasn't every single night, but usually three or four nights a week. Because we were working together, and we were all so good at the detailed side of things, the role-plays were getting more graphic and less cartoonish.

People also loved role-playing with me because I was a good writer. At times, I would cater more to their kicks and fetishes during a role-play. There would be more focus on blood and gore, or feet, or whatever they wanted to be into.

I also got messages from users who said they were women, and they wanted to do a role-play or a story where I was the captor and they were the victim, but I was not into that. It just was not my thing. What really turned me on were role-plays involving the women I knew. As we got into the role-plays, I was able to envision how the woman would sound as she was gagged, or how she would look with an apple in her mouth. As odd it may sound to someone not in the scene, all it was to me was a bunch of people exchanging similar interests, or similar ideas. It was obvious that it was all fantasy. These were things that were supposedly taking place in a [nonexistent] mountain house in the middle of nowhere. Sometimes they would even be "taking place" on another continent.

A few of my role-play partners suggested that we chat away

from DFN because the website was pretty slow, so I created a Yahoo Messenger account. I chatted and role-played with my favorites on Yahoo. It was instant communication, and picture sharing was a lot easier. I also had all of my favorites in one spot, and I could tell when they were online. I would still connect with more people on DFN and if I thought I would like role-playing with them, I shared my Yahoo Messenger name with them. Early in 2012, Yahoo Messenger became my primary way to chat and role-play with people who I had connected with on DFN.

My typical scenario was pretty standard. Sometimes, someone would give me a new idea for a new bondage position, or something of that nature, and if I liked it, I would incorporate it. The things I got into the most were when my partner and I were talking about a plan to go about kidnapping a woman, and, of course, the part where she is stripped and tied up. That was pretty much where my kink ended. From there, I kind of let my role-play partner take it where he or she wanted and I would play along.

If someone was able to get detailed with the role-plays, then I really would get into it. Some guys tried, but they just couldn't pull it off. I am a decent writer and was proud of my own scenarios. It was pretty much always around kidnapping and bondage. If I liked the way the other user wrote, sometimes we would tailor the story towards what he or she was interested in. Some of the people I chatted with were more into blood, gore, and torture, which generally didn't turn me on. Other people enjoyed a slavery scenario, where the kidnapped woman would be put up for auction and sold to the highest bidder. I started to enjoy that theme more and more, so I began to incorporate it. When I created new albums, I would title them "Cook Her or Sell Her?" The photos were always of women I knew in real life, including Kathleen.

The whole thing was like this big fantasy group, like a group of guys getting together to play Dungeons and Dragons, or World of Warcraft. Except in our case we weren't talking about rogues and mages and the spells they could cast, we were talking about kidnapping women, and sometimes killing them too. Not quite the thing that would ever be a huge success with the masses.

I thought I had balanced all of this with my real life easily and had settled into what I considered to be a very successful life. I had passed the NYPD sergeant's exam, my job was challenging and frustrating, but with the upcoming promotion things were looking up and I was making good money. While our relationship was not perfect, Kathleen and I had a good marriage by anyone's definition, we were in love, and were both thrilled about the baby.

5.

My daily routine was pretty much the same as it had been. I was down for anything as long as Kathleen was happy. She loved penguins, so in 2012, on our only Mother's Day together, we had a family day at the Bronx Zoo. I loved how Kathleen held our daughter as she pointed at the animals, slowly naming them.

Sometimes, when I had a day off, she would go out and have some alone time for herself or go out with friends. I would either stay home with the baby or go out with her and take her to the park. I only had eleven months with the baby before she was taken from me. I was looking forward to her starting to talk. She would mumble "dadadada" before "mamamama." When she started saying "dada," Kathleen would laugh and play with her and say "MOMMA MOMMA" really slow. I knew that physiologically it is easier for a baby to pronounce "Dada," but it was still a fun thing Kathleen and I laughed about.

While I was comfortable with who I was and did not internally feel any shame, I still felt that my sexual fetishes were the kind of thing that I should never talk to anyone about. I felt the same way about bringing this up to Kathleen. She was my wife and she was my friend, but it honestly never even occurred to me to tell her my fantasies. It wasn't an issue to me. I was fine with conventional sex. I was often totally caught up in the pleasure of the moment when I made love to her, so I rarely ever thought about my darker fantasies when

I was with her. Every once in a while, I would imagine her tied to the bed while we were having sex, but that was about it. I just kept doing what I had always done, what just about everyone does, which was to keep my fantasies secret from my real life.

The sex with Kathleen, though pretty "vanilla" was always good, so I didn't need to have her tied up to enjoy sex with her. I didn't want to risk really freaking her out. I didn't think telling her about the stuff I was into would go over so well. But it wasn't just that I didn't tell her. I didn't tell anyone. They were my own private thoughts that I shared with screen names on the Internet. I didn't even need to do that. I had gone my whole life before DFN. But since I found a place where other people were into some of the same stuff, I enjoyed it from time to time.

Whatever the case, I thought that everything was fine just the way it was. Maybe somewhere down the road I would have coyly mentioned something to Kathleen about trying a little bondage stuff, but we'll never know.

Until I found the Dark Fetish Network, I never realized quite how many people were into this sort of thing. It was not that I thought anything was wrong with me; I was just aroused by certain things, just like everyone else. Just because my template was different didn't mean I thought that it was a big problem. I would never harm anyone in real life, so why did I care what turned me on?

This was my thing, so I was not particularly ashamed, not any more than any normal guy looking at porn at would be. On DFN, I was normal. In fact, I was tame, compared to some of them, a lot of the people on that site were into some really wild stuff.

The sharing of women's' Facebook photos was not an idea that originated with me, it was something that I learned on the site. That practice was fairly common on DFN. Looking back on all of this, the graphic chats and role-plays were one thing, but the sharing of the Facebook photos is something I did that really bothers me. When I was just an anonymous screen name, I wasn't always circumspect and obviously I never imagined that anyone would find out what was going on. The pictures were used as props, and they were a contribution of mine to fellow users. I thought the women I knew were attractive and I figured that others might think so too. But still, I should not have done it. Was it illegal? Certainly not. Was it crossing these women's personal boundaries and even an invasion of their privacy? Yes, and for that I feel terrible.

Some people would later argue that I was planning real crimes because all of this involved women that I knew in real life. If you think about your own sexual fantasies, I would think that you often fantasize about people you know too, and you don't ask them if it would be okay to do so. That is how it goes; a guy that is into vanilla sex might fantasize about having sex with his wife's best friend. A guy with a female boss might think a lot about having her on her knees in front of him. Well, it was the same thing with me; the only difference was that my fantasies were not quite so vanilla.

As long as the role-play involved some kind of kidnapping and bondage I was generally okay with it. When it came to my cannibalism fetish things remained the same and had not progressed into blood and gore. I never got to the part where I was actually eating the person. The idea of the girl tied up and being prepared to be cooked was the peak of it, what I was into was the image of a woman tied up on a platter with an apple in her mouth, not the act itself.

Around June 2012, I started getting a lot of messages from a guy from England. His screen name was MoodyBlues. He would message me, we would chat about our mutual kink and then I would often send a photo of a woman I knew. We exchanged Yahoo Messenger screen names and we got into it. We hatched a fantasy scheme of how he would come to the U.S. and we would kidnap all of these women and we would have a cookout. We took turns coming up with new ideas about what we could do to our helpless victims.

One of the people we talked about a lot was Kate, the woman I knew from Maryland. I had fantasized about her a lot over the years and he liked her. He and I would talk about Kate and make up stories of what we would do to her. Sometimes we would just start all over and make up a new storyline, other times we would abandon her for a bit and pick a new girl, but we always came back to her. In real life Kate and I still kept in touch and we were still close friends. Every time I traveled down to Maryland, we would get together.

MoodyBlues and I had been chatting about her for quite awhile, well before I made any plans to go to Maryland. In the middle of July 2012, I was on vacation from work, so Kathleen and I decided we would spend a long weekend down in Maryland. She loved the Maryland campus and it would be the first time my college friends got to see my daughter.

I sent out a text message to all of my friends in Maryland letting them know I was coming down and to let me know if they want to get together. Kate was one of the people that responded. She texted, "Lunch Sunday?" I said sure and then she picked the time and the place.

The next time I chatted with MoodyBlues we continued our story about her and I mentioned that I was actually going to see her this coming weekend. He made a couple of stupid jokes about me thinking about her as the meal instead of the actual meal we ordered. Then we just continued on with the role-play.

We drove down on Friday and hung out at my friend's place with our kids. On Saturday we went to over to see some of my other friends then walked around the Maryland campus. I bought my daughter a little baby Maryland Terps hat. For dinner we drove into Rockville. There are a lot of restaurants on this strip called Rockville Pike and it was pretty close to the hotel. We ended up settling for Chili's and on the way there I drove by Kate's office building, which is enormous, and also pink. I mentioned it to Kathleen, something like, "The girl we're meeting tomorrow works in this pink building." So when we got to Chili's, I took a minute to text Kate and confirm tomorrow's plans, and I also said, "Oh, and by the way, we drove by your pink building." She responded, "Yay!"

We all met for brunch and had a really nice time. Kate held the baby and played with her. Kathleen and Kate hit it off. When we left and we were getting back in the car, Kathleen asked if Kate and I were ever together in college. She probably saw the chemistry between us. I said no, it never worked out. Kathleen said she was surprised and said that Kate was totally my type of girl, and that she could have seen us being together.

When I got back, I told MoodyBlues how delicious and great she looked and then we moved on to something else. It was my turn to help him out for a bit. Some of these guys might be into something I wasn't into, but we would take turns helping each other out. My role-play partners knew it was fantasy, of course, even if we did not say that all the time. If we had just keep saying every three lines that it was just a fantasy, the whole thing would not have worked, it would have broken the spell.

During the summer of 2012, my computer broke down and I started using Kathleen's. I had my own account and my own login. At first, I stayed away from my usual habits because I was too nervous to surf porn on her computer because I didn't want to get busted, but then after a while it was just business as usual and I started back up with my use of porn. One day, about two weeks before she left for good, I forgot to log off and she saw one of the bondage sites I was into. It was not DFN, but was regular bondage, something like a woman tied up in restraints with a ball gag in her mouth. While this was tame to me, it was obviously a bit shocking to her.

I woke up to her tapping my shoulder. It was around eight a.m. She looked really nervous, she kept trying to look me in the eye, but couldn't quite do it. I immediately could tell something was really wrong. She said that I left the computer logged into my account, and though she didn't mean to open it, she did and it was on some website with a woman tied up. She wasn't confrontational, she seemed legit nervous. I sat next to her and my mind was racing.

I gave her a really watered down version of what I was in to. I apologized first and said I never meant for her to see that, but it was really nothing. I told her that sometimes I come home from work and I'm really wound up but I don't want to wake her up so I look at porn. I told her that I just look at regular stuff, but once in awhile I look at bondage websites. The thing she found was just a regular bondage website. I don't remember which one it was. Whatever it was, there wasn't anything crazy violent on there, so I was able to massage it down and just tell her that I had been aroused by some bondage stuff. I was extremely relieved that she had not found any of the heavier things I was involved with.

What I said seemed to calm her down and she said that it was okay, and that she understood. She said she had been thinking of ways to spice up our sex life, and that maybe this would be a way to do it. She talked a bit about how she would be willing to try a little light bondage, and said that maybe we could get some supplies at a sex shop and experiment just a little.

While it was embarrassing as hell, this conversation went way better than I expected. I was really excited, because despite all of my fantasizing, I had never engaged in anything resembling my fantasies in real life. Later that day while I was at work, she texted me, "Go to the shop by the west 4th subway stop. I'm sure it's open late. Handcuffs, silk scarves..."

I never went to the sex shop. I couldn't work up my nerve to go in. This had all just been fantasy my whole life and I was intimidated to go into a physical store and buy some of the toys we had agreed upon. The thought of going up to the counter and paying for these things filled me with the same sort of anxiety that I used to feel as a little kid back in school. In retrospect, I know we could have just used a sheet or a pillowcase or something, but doing it in real life was totally new to me. I honestly didn't know how to start. It seemed so awkward to do anything like this with Kathleen. It sounded sexy, but could I really engage in this side of my sexual life with her? Or even with anyone? It wasn't that I thought if I started that I would not be able to stop, it was more just totally foreign to me to think about doing any of this stuff in real life. Maybe in a couple of weeks I would have gone in, but we'll never know.

It turned out that me not going to the sex shop was a part of my downfall, but it also turned out to be a blessing. She installed spyware on the computer about two weeks after our talk. I found out later she installed the spyware because she thought I was having an affair. I can only surmise that she grew suspicious when I didn't go to the sex shop and she suspected that there might have been someone else I was involved with. This, of course, led to her finding the kind of pornography I was really looking at and eventually all the chats that went along with the secret fantasy life I was living.

Not going into the sex shop was also a blessing because had I purchased some items to restrain her during consensual sex, the FBI would have found them after arresting me and they undoubtedly would have considered that evidence that I had crossed the line from fantasy to reality.

I wasn't a perfect husband or a perfect father but I was improving at both. I was very excited about our future together. On August 30, 2012, twelve days before Kathleen left for good, I attended a party in honor of my precinct's Commanding Officer getting promoted. One of the female officers drank way too much and she was getting sick. The guy who said he was going to drive her home didn't want to leave yet and everyone was trying to figure out what to do with her. I took it upon myself to make the call. I decided to take her home immediately and to spend the night on her couch to make sure she made it through the night okay.

I texted Kathleen to let her know what was going on. She texted me back; "I'm proud that you're the kind of man who will take care of his friends even if it's really inconvenient. Love u :)"

On the morning of September 10th, 12 days after she sent that text message, she woke me up in the exact same way as she did a couple of weeks prior and said, "I logged into the computer just now and I saw everything."

The timing of this was amazingly screwed up. I had actually closed out my DFN account just the night before. Who knows if I would have gone back to it, but I had decided to not do it anymore. The baby was going to turn one soon and she would be walking. I was staying up late and tired at work because of chatting all the time with MoodyBlues, the guy from England. After Kathleen caught me the first time, I didn't want to go through that again. After I closed my account I messaged MoodyBlues on Yahoo Messenger and told him I had closed out DFN. He asked why, and I said jokingly, "Less of a chance of getting caught."

Although I closed out DFN and swore off the role-plays, I did still look at some BDSM and cannibal-related pornography the night she installed spyware on our computer. When she woke me up this time, at first I tried playing dumb, but she gave a sarcastic laugh and said, "Oh, so you're going to deny it?" and she walked away. She seemed less nervous this time, and more unhinged. Her eyes looked like those of a wounded animal. I got out of bed and followed her down the hall and just kept saying her name over and over. I wanted to talk to her, but she cut me off and said, "Cook women? Grill them? That's what we are to you?"

I was wondering what the hell she saw, but I knew whatever it was, it was not good. The odds ranged from really bad to Doomsday catastrophic.

She said, "Look, I already called my parents. I'm going to take the baby and just get away for a while. "

I started to ask her not to leave. I said, "Kathleen, what you saw is not who I am."

She started crying, and kept saying, "No."

I told her that I loved her and she kept crying harder and saying, "No." That's all she kept saying for awhile. She looked incredibly sad and hurt.

I was mortified. I just kept repeating that she knows me, and I kept apologizing. I had no idea what she saw but I knew she did some computer tricks and that she must have seen one of the cannibalism forums or websites that I looked at.

I kept begging her not to go. I didn't know what to say. I was embarrassed of course, but I was still Gil. I was still her husband, I was still the man she fell in love with, and I loved her. I hated that this was happening and it was all my fault.

She got up and went to the bedroom, opened up the closet, and started packing. I stood there watching her. I asked her again not to go. She was a little calmer at this point.

She stopped and looked at me and said "Look, this isn't goodbye forever. I am just a little freaked out and I need to get away."

I decided to back off for now and not dig myself a deeper hole. She told me to watch the baby and feed her while she packed. I held my daughter. I was beyond dejected. I kept thinking about how I was going to explain this to my parents. "Hey, Mom and Dad, Kathleen found me looking at cannibal porn and took off with the baby," did not sound like it was going to fly.

She packed her stuff while I fed the baby lunch. Then she said she was going to wait downstairs at the apartment of a friend who was going to drive her to the airport. I asked her one more time to please not go, but she wasn't having it. She left the apartment with the baby and all of her stuff and walked down the hall. I left the door open and just stood there. She waited by the elevator and burst out crying, louder than she had all morning. From the time she woke me up, to the time she walked out the door, probably only about ninety minutes had passed.

She texted me as soon as she left, "I do love you."

Later on, she sent another one: "We are going to figure this out. I'm not giving up. Something u can do is find a good couples therapist covered by GHI. Maybe make an appointment for a couple of weeks. What do you think?"

I responded, "Sounds great I am happy to hear that. When you come back we start over that's it. I never want to see you like that again and I won't let it happen again."

I was humiliated beyond belief. It had never occurred to me that this day would come, or that Kathleen would be frightened or scared of me. But that text message exchange after she left gave me hope that we would be okay. We had been friends a long time. We loved each other. I knew this was hard for her to grasp, but once she calmed down it would be okay.

When she was gone, I went into damage control. There was no way that I could tell my parents what really happened so I made up a story that her father had some health problems and she had to go be with him in Nevada. They bought it for a few weeks, but it became obvious that something was wrong when we missed the baby's first birthday.

I wasn't sure if she had just found that I was on the site, or if she had read everything that I had written, and seen the photos. Needless to say I was in a panic. At one point she texted me and asked me if I ever used pictures of her or our daughter on the site. Of course I never used our daughter but I lied to her and said I never used pictures of her. I didn't tell her the truth at the time because I didn't want to hurt her anymore, and I was afraid of how she would react. If I told her I used pictures of her, I thought she might want a divorce.

Other than that, I was honest, and told her everything. In my mind I knew I had done something wrong, but I also knew who she was, and I thought she knew who I was. As miserable as I was, in one way it was nice to let it out and to be honest with my wife.

I sent her a message every couple of days. I wanted to know how she and the baby were doing. She only wanted text messages. She said she couldn't handle hearing my voice for the time being. I asked her when she was coming back. She never gave an answer. She said she couldn't give an answer. She kept asking me to come clean on everything, so I did. Little pieces at first, but eventually I literally told her everything, about how I was sending pictures on the Internet, role-playing about doing things to women that I knew.

I was a total mess. I couldn't sleep, I couldn't eat. I was losing a ton of weight. I hated being home because everything was a reminder of how things used to be, and how they were not anymore. The baby's play area was just as she left it, all her toys were there. I couldn't handle picking it up or moving things around.

To avoid being home when I was really depressed, I slept at the precinct some nights. I did as much overtime as I could, anything not to be home. My police friends didn't even know she had left. I was keeping all of it inside. How could I explain to anyone why she had gone?

I could see that my wife might not want me after she found out that part of me, but I just kept telling myself that she needed some space and that we would work this out when she came back.

At this point, I thought things were as bad as they possibly could get. I had hurt my wife, I was humiliated in front of her, and she had left me. But I had no idea what was coming next.

6.

I was off from work. October 24th seemed like just another day, which these days was not a good thing. My depression was deepening, it was becoming harder and harder for me to deal with Kathleen taking the baby and leaving me. When she first left, she had guessed it would be about two weeks before she came back. Now she couldn't give me an answer. That morning, like every other morning, the first thing I did when I woke up was check my phone to see if Kathleen had texted me. Nothing. I hated bugging her and asking if she knew when she was going to come back home, but I thought I might ask again today. It had been a few days since I had done so last. I walked Dudley, fed him, then sat on the couch and put on The Godfather.

At about 2 p.m., there was a knock on the door. Dudley barked once, but I didn't move. I wasn't expecting any visitors and didn't want to talk to anyone. The knock came again, and, once again, I ignored it. I figured it was the mail lady. Sometimes when my mailbox was full, she would bring everything upstairs for me. I hadn't checked my mail in a while, so that had to be it. The knocking stopped.

Two minutes later, I got a text from Kathleen.

"Thanks for sending the video of Dudley in the park. We were all laughing."

That made me smile. I wrote back and asked her how she was doing. Just then, the phone rang. It was from an

"Unknown" number. I ignored it. No voicemail was left but 5 minutes later the Unknown number called again. This time I answered.

A male voice said, "Hello, is this Officer Valle?"

"Yes, who's this?"

He explained that he was Officer "So and so" from the 112th Precinct. He said that my parked car had just been hit, and that the damage was pretty bad. He said, "Just come down and we'll do the report."

I was pissed off. As if I didn't have enough crap going on, now my car was struck while it was just sitting there. It didn't seem possible for life to get much worse. I put on a ragged red Maryland T-shirt, jeans, and sneakers, holstered up my gun at my side, and headed for the door.

"I'll be right back, buddy," I said to Dudley.

My apartment was all the way at the end of the hall, so upon leaving the apartment, I made a quick left to head for the stairs when I saw six men in the hallway with guns pointed at me.

"Put your hands up," the lead guy said calmly. I immediately knew what this was about. It had to be about my computer activities. There was nothing else going on.

"Put your hands against the wall," the man said as they made their way towards me. I told myself it was all a misunderstanding. Just stay calm, do what they say and it'll be okay.

One of them cuffed my hands behind my back and asked where my gun was. I told him it was at my right hip. The agent took the gun and handed it to one of the other guys. Then a guy in a suit came up to me. He was a young guy, but looked like he was the one in charge.

"Gil, do you want to go back inside the apartment so we can talk?"

I said yes. What else could I say? They took the key out of my pocket and we all went into the apartment. Dudley barked once, and a couple of the guys walked over to pet him and he mellowed out fast. Kathleen and I always joked that Dudley is so dumb and friendly that if burglars ever came in, he would want to play with them. Now, there he was playing with guys who just pointed guns at my chest. The agent with the suit put his hand on my shoulder.

"Everything is going to be alright."

"I don't think so," I responded.

Although I tried to maintain a calm demeanor, my heart was racing. It had only been about three minutes since I had six guns pointed at me and I was in handcuffs. While my apartment was being searched, I was thinking about Kathleen and my family. It was all impossible to process. Internally, I was already a mess, and everything was not going to be all right, but those four simple words I had just uttered to the FBI agent would later come back to haunt me.

The agent continued, "We're going to just talk, alright? We're not even going to go to the main office. We're going to go to an annex, and we're just going to talk."

That calmed me down a bit. Talking was okay. I tried to tell myself that if I explained everything, they would understand it and let me go. It wasn't like I had actually done anything, certainly nothing that would warrant six guys coming to arrest me. Obviously there was some sort of enormous misunderstanding going on for them to send six agents to my apartment. A very small part of me was actually looking forward to just getting all of this off of my chest, even if it was to an FBI agent. I was innocent, and knew the agent would be able to see that. How could anyone not see that? I hadn't done anything.

I asked for two favors before they left. "Can we leave in a way that no one in the building would know?" The agent in the suit said that wouldn't be a problem.

My second favor was "Can one of you guys put food in my dog's bowl and make sure he has enough water?" I told one of them where the food was kept, and they didn't have a problem with that either.

"It's okay buddy," I said one more time to Dudley. This would be the last time I would see him for 21 months.

They walked me out of the building and put me in the back seat of a black SUV and I was taken to lower Manhattan. I did my best to breathe slowly and keep my composure, but it wasn't easy. There was still no official mention that I was being arrested, or why. I thought it was possible that I was just being brought in to be questioned. Just because I was handcuffed did not necessarily mean I was under arrest. I would just explain it to them and they would get that it was all fantasy. They'd tell me to cut it out, which I already did, and move on with my life. I was law enforcement like them. They wouldn't be out to get me.

The driver pulled into a garage somewhere in lower Manhattan. We got out of the car and the agent with the suit approached me again. He asked if I would give them permission to search my NYPD locker.

"Sure, go ahead," I said.

The agent got on his cell phone to call someone, who I assumed was at my precinct. There was nothing out of the ordinary in my locker. There were just uniforms, a police belt, and a whole mess of copies of summonses that I had written over the last handful of years.

They walked me into an elevator, and then through a maze of hallways until we got into an interview room. The agent who originally seized my firearm was there and he casually placed the gun on the table. It was definitely a mistake on their part because as a cop you would never leave someone you are about to question with a loaded firearm. They took the cuffs off of me and asked if I wanted a cup of coffee. I said yes, and they sent some young guy out for coffee. Then they left me alone with my loaded gun on the table. I sat there for a bit, alone with my thoughts. How many people know? Does Kathleen know? How was I going to explain this to her and my family? Do my coworkers know?

I stared at my gun while I tried to stay calm. I would have a chance to explain myself. It would be embarrassing, sure it would, but they would get it and I would be back home later.

The guy with the suit came back in along with another agent who took the gun away. The lead agent shook my hand and formally introduced himself. His name was Anthony Foto. He said, "For a year and a half we've been monitoring your computer activities. This is your chance now to sort of get ahead in the game and give us a chance to understand the human element of all of this. Right now, all we have to go off is this stuff."

He pointed to a box full of papers. I nodded, and he continued: "If you choose to go the lawyer route, we won't have a chance to understand any of this. I would take this as your opportunity to help us understand all of this."

I stopped him and said that I didn't need a lawyer. I told him this was all a misunderstanding and that I would explain it all. I didn't want to have it all held up by a lawyer. Of course people didn't understand, but as soon as I told them about how it was all just fantasy, just a game I played to get off, then they would get it and let me go.

One thing I've heard a lot since that day is something like, "You were a cop. You, of all people, should know that you don't talk to the police without a lawyer." I understood that, but as an innocent man I had nothing to hide. In my mind, I was thinking that if I lawyered up it would look like I was hiding something. In my wildest dreams, I could not imagine how much my words were going to be twisted. The first hour was easy. I talked about my upbringing and covered basically everything from childhood to my days in the NYPD. No talk about Dark Fetish Net, just relatively boring stuff.

After all of the routine stuff, he produced a piece of paper. It was my Miranda rights. Before he started to ask questions about the computer activities, I had to document that I had been read my rights and that I waived my right to have a lawyer present during questioning. I signed away my rights, and we got started. Foto asked about my relationship with one of the women who I role played about, who would later be deemed to be one of the so-called "victims." It all seemed like a nightmare.

That's how it went for much of the next two hours. Foto would name one of the women and I would tell him all about my relationship with her. There was nothing that I did with any of them that wasn't completely innocent in real life. After we covered the women, he got a little more specific. He started to ask me more about Dark Fetish Net and my interactions on there. I told him that it was all make-believe. I also acknowledged that a few of the people sounded more serious than others. It seemed like this was the kind of thing I should say at this moment. Why else was I in FBI custody? I went on to explain that some of the stories and role-plays sounded a little more realistic, but they were still make-believe.

As he laid it all out, things continued to get more detailed and looked a whole lot worse. It was becoming very apparent that the FBI had spent a lot of time investigating this. He went on to ask me about the role-play scenarios as they pertained to each woman. It was difficult to explain to him why I used Facebook photos of real women, mainly because I was embarrassed to tell him that I did it because it turned me on. I told him that I did it, but that it was all fake. The personal information I sent about the women wasn't accurate except for their first names.

Foto then asked me if, at any point, any of the computer activities crossed over into my real life. This seemed easy, but I didn't want to slip up and just say "no" because I was afraid it would make me seem less than honest. So I told him "no", but that when I talked to the guy from England the fantasy life and real life crossed lines a bit because I stayed up later to talk to him. So maybe in that sense, because I was staying up later, the fantasy life "was bleeding into" my personal life. On nights that I role-played with him, I stayed up a little later than usual and was waking up more tired the next day. As much as this was an awful experience, I had hope as I was able to definitively say that there were no real world actions despite everything that was said in the chats about me conducting surveillance and trying to figure out the best opportunity to kidnap one of these women. Then he hit me with something that I was not expecting. He said that the day after he had had an online chat about one of the women, "We have you on her block."

Now I was freaking out. I knew that I wasn't actually stalking women, but I was not doubting an FBI agent saying that their technology placed me on a woman's block. I knew it was a coincidence, and I knew generally where the woman we were talking about lived. I was scrambling through my mental Rolodex; what was I doing on that block? I didn't even have a date to work off of. I had to blindly explain why I was on a particular block without being able to reference anything.

Then, all of a sudden, I remembered that one day I had dropped Kathleen and the baby off in that woman's area so that they could have lunch. Sometimes I would drive Kathleen to Manhattan on my way to work. I breathed a huge sigh of relief. I remembered waving to the woman too before I drove off. That had to be it. It obviously was completely innocent, and not related to any fake conspiracy to kidnap her. I happily told the agent the information, glad that I could legitimately explain it away.

As it turned out I was half correct. The date that the FBI had in mind was March 1, 2012. Sometime after the interview it appears that either Foto or one of the prosecutors called Kathleen and the woman and asked them if they had lunch on March 1st. Both of them said no, so the conclusion they drew was that I lied to them. Later during the trial, both of them testified that I actually had dropped Kathleen off for lunch with that woman, but neither one could remember the date. I was expected to pinpoint and perfectly explain when that lunch was between them without having any date to work off of, while Kathleen and the other woman had weeks to prepare for the trial, yet neither one of them could remember when the lunch took place. To the FBI and the prosecutors there could be no other explanation. To them, I lied.

But still, where was I on March 1st? They still had me on the woman's block on that date. According to my work records, I was assigned to the counter terrorism unit with my sergeant that day, so the whole city was my beat. I could have been anywhere. Moreover, the phone call I made that placed me "on her very block" was made to Kathleen. A friend of hers had given birth at a hospital nearby so I took a break from work and drove over to the hospital. Kathleen came downstairs with our daughter and they met my sergeant for the first time. Kathleen and the sergeant both confirmed this meeting at trial.

The interview was over. In closing, Foto asked me if I would be willing to help the FBI determine who might be doing real crime on DFN. I was willing and told him that it would be tough, but I would agree to help them with whatever they needed. He said the one condition on the deal was that if I had just lied to him about anything that would be off the table.

"If I find out that you lied, or that there are other instances of surveillance, I am going to be disappointed," he said.

The word "other" jumped out at me. I thought I had just cleared that up. There was no surveillance. I told him that everything that I said was the truth.

Foto said that he was going to reach out to the Assistant U.S. Attorney [AUSA] and tell her that they weren't "dealing with the big bad wolf." That put me at ease again for a moment, and then he continued. "But for now, we have to get you booked and all of that. You know the drill. Do you even know what you are being charged with?" he asked.

After spending four hours talking about bondage and cannibalism fantasies, I took a stab at it. "Conspiracy to commit murder?"

"Conspiracy to commit kidnapping," he corrected me.

At trial he testified that the first thing he asked me in the interview room was did I know why I was there. He said I responded, "Conspiracy to commit murder." Unfortunately, this whole interview was not recorded. They argued that since that was the first question and that's how I answered it, it showed that I had a guilty mind. Although the interview wasn't recorded another agent was taking notes. His handwritten notes were detailed and chronological. Nowhere in his notes is the date "March 1" written, and the question Foto asked me about whether or not I knew what I was being charged with is one of the last things written in the notes. That's the best proof I have that he lied on the stand.

With the interview over, I was walked to another part of the building so I could be photographed and fingerprinted. It had been about five hours since I was taken out of my apartment. I began wondering if anyone knew what was going on. It was real now. I was being arrested. People thought that the fantasies I was writing about late at night to get off might actually be true. How did this happen?

I held out hope that Foto would talk to the AUSA and convince her to drop the case. He was being nice enough, civil at least, and I had explained everything to him truthfully and honestly. There was no way there was any real case here, there was no proof of anything. It had to be dropped. Maybe Kathleen and my family would never even find out about it and I could just go back to normal life.

They hadn't offered me a chance to call anyone during that entire interview, but I am not sure I would have. Who in my life would I call and let know that something like this had happened? The police union never showed up, which I thought was odd. They provide representation for cops who had been caught drunk driving and others who had been arrested for domestic assault and such things, but to this point, nothing for those with cannibal fetishes.

I was fingerprinted and put in the back of the same SUV that we arrived in. The driver was the only agent in the car with me. He wasn't part of the interview, but he was at my apartment and he drove the SUV earlier. He broke the silence. "Gil, do you want to call someone in your family to pick up the dog?"

I thanked the agent but said no, and that I would deal with that after the court hearing tomorrow. I figured Dudley might have crapped in the house, but I would be out on bail after he saw the judge, and then I would deal with the mess from there. The last thing I wanted to do was let anyone know where I was right now.

Soon we arrived at the rear of the prison. Agent Foto and another agent, Rocky Warden, were in another car following us. We were informed that the prison was currently on lock down for the nightly count and they weren't taking anyone in for about an hour. There was nothing to do but wait.

"The Giants are winning." The driver of the SUV checked

his phone and gave me the update on Game 1 of the World Series. It made me think of my dad. We had watched so much baseball growing up together, and if he didn't know what was going on yet, he was definitely watching the ball game. The shock of what had happened was lessening and a deep sadness was taking over.

Foto came up to the car and told the driver they could put me in his car so that I wouldn't have to wait around anymore. They moved me to the back of a beige minivan. "Hey, great job," Foto told the driver of the SUV. They shook hands, congratulating each other for arresting me.

Not much else was said for the rest of the night. Eventually I was walked into the prison and became in the custody of the Federal Bureau of Prisons [BOP]. I was now inmate #91921-054. I was absolutely mentally exhausted. I felt nervous for sure, but I was still was looking forward to the chance to clear this all up. Maybe the AUSA would come through after hearing about the post- arrest interview. I had to fill out a bunch of paperwork for the BOP. One of the questions was whether or not general population would be an issue for me. I checked "yes," and wrote down that I was an active police officer. None of the prison officers said a word to me the whole night. They brought me to a strip search area. I took off all of my civilian clothes. They made me lift up my ball sack, turn around, bend over, the whole thing. It was beyond mortifying.

I was brought upstairs to the SHU, the Special Housing Unit, which is the place where they keep people not allowed in general population for any number of reasons, and put in a cell alone. I lay down in bed right away, and tried to gather my thoughts. I was exhausted and I wanted to try to get some rest, but I couldn't. The whole thing hadn't really registered with me yet. My mind kept circling back over the whole day, and I kept trying to figure out what I was going to do when I got out of court in the morning. I thought about the media and how if they found out about this, it was going to be all over the news. I thought, crap, they are probably going to call me "The Cannibal Cop." Even with all of my worrying, I still couldn't grasp how big this was.

I slept little, if at all, and was startled by a hard knock on the door.

"Get ready for court," a female officer yelled.

Get ready? How? I had a prison jumpsuit on. No toothbrush, no razor, no nothing. I was ready. About 30 minutes later, they opened up a slot in the middle of the door and told me to turn around and put my hands through the slot. They cuffed me before opening the door and pulled me out. They brought me downstairs, handed me my red Maryland shirt and jeans, and then they put me in another cell.

Some time later, the door opened and there was Agent Foto, along with the Agent Warden, who was the one who left the loaded gun on the table the day before. They said good morning but I got right down to business and asked them if they talked to the AUSA.

The answer was no. "We're having a meeting later this morning, but for now we're supposed to go to court." I went along with them, not saying much. Warden handed me a brown bag.

"That's for you."

There was a sandwich inside, but I told him I didn't want it. I couldn't eat.

"Are you sure? It's probably going to be a really long day."

I didn't want it, so he put it on a desk and we all walked out of the prison into another car. They put me in the back seat and they took a short drive to another building. Foto was in the passenger's seat. He turned around and asked me a question.

"Are you alright? How are you feeling?"

"Nervous and terrified."

"I can understand."

That was all that was said. They took me out of the car, walked me into the next building, and put me in another interview room, took the handcuffs off and left me there. A few minutes later, a young woman came in and sat opposite from me. She identified herself as someone from Pre-Trial Services.

She asked me some questions, I don't recall about what. I was using my hands while I was talking to her. She interrupted me coldly and sternly, "Please keep your hands on your lap." She believed that I was a danger. She wanted no part of being in that room with me. All of a sudden, I had become a dangerous man. I answered what I had to answer and signed what I had to sign. She left and I was alone for a few minutes again. Then another woman walked in. She was professional looking, wearing a skirt and high heels.

"These are very serious allegations," were the first words out of her mouth as she made her way in and sat opposite from me. She identified herself as Julia Gatto from the public defender's office.

"Look, I read the complaint a few times. I totally get it. It's like a game, right? You're not actually out there munching on women's legs."

Yeah, she got it right away. I gave her the cliff notes version of what happened. She wanted to know how much I told the FBI.

"I told them everything. I'm innocent."

She was obviously disappointed, but she said to me that would be dealt with later. She said, "Alright, we're going to have a bail hearing soon, but you're not going to get bail. Eventually though, we'll keep applying for bail and once this all kind of dies down, I think you'll make bail."

I thanked her for being straight with me.

"I never sugar coat things with my clients. I don't think it helps. I'll probably sugar coat it for your family though."

Apply for bail when this all died down? When all what died down? I wasn't going to get bail? I knew that sometimes even people that *had* killed people got bail of some sort. This seemed worse and worse as time went on.

Worst of all was the terror that I felt about what my wife and family would think. Kathleen might never want me back if she found this out. I asked Julia if she had talked with anyone in my family yet. She said no, and took down some phone numbers. The first one I gave her was Kathleen's. I asked her to please tell my wife that it was all a misunderstanding and that it would work itself out. As much as I was fearful of her reaction, some small part of me thought she might come home at this point, to help support me through this.

"Hang in there and I'll see you soon," she said before leaving the room.

Foto and Warden were waiting outside. I was cuffed and taken to the hallway. Foto asked me what I thought about Julia, and before I answered, he opined that she seemed pretty good.

I ignored his comment and just blurted out, "This is going to kill my family."

He didn't say anything else as they walked me down to another area, into another holding cell where I sat for around five hours until Julia showed up again and talked to me through the bars.

"We're going in soon, okay?" She told me that my family was there, and that they were supportive, that they don't believe any of the allegations. This did not make me happy; I didn't want my family there to hear what had happened and what I had been accused of.

I then asked, "Did you talk to my wife?"

The response was not what I expected. "Yes I did. She sounded very angry with you. She said she wasn't going to help."

I had still not figured out that it was Kathleen that dropped a dime on me in the first place. I hadn't made the connection yet. Everything was too much for me to grasp. Julia left and, a few minutes later, two U.S. Marshalls showed up and opened up the cell door.

One said, "Dude, have you ever been to federal court before?"

I said, "No."

He said "Okay, it is really unbelievably crowded in there, I have never seen anything like it. Just look straight ahead, and sit at the table with your attorney."

I took a deep breath, and they walked me down the hall. They opened the door at the end, and I entered the side of the courtroom. It was packed. Standing room only. I tried to find my family in the crowd, but I didn't see them. I sat right next to Julia and she explained to me what was going to happen in court.

Then she said, "Some of the papers are reporting that your wife was cooperating with the feds. Do you...." she started to ask me, but was interrupted when the judge entered. Suddenly everything got quiet. Everything was happening so fast. My mind reeled. Kathleen had something to do with this?

The bail hearing began with the prosecutor, Hadassa Waxman, standing up and laying out the case, and arguing why I shouldn't get bail. I heard the words, but they didn't make sense: ".... abduct, rape, torture, and cannibalize a number of women who he knew in real life."

I also heard her say the words, "....faces life in prison."

At this point, my mind was exploding. Waxman went on and explained that this was not just a computer crime, that this was something that I was planning to do, and would have done if I was not arrested. I sat there stunned. She stated that I took numerous real world steps to carry out this plot. I had driven all the way down to Maryland to see a woman who I had targeted. The woman claimed that she thought it was incredibly weird that, out of nowhere, I would want to come from New York to see her, because I hadn't seen her or talked to her in so long. Allegedly, I also stalked a woman, while in my uniform, in my patrol car "in a very intimidating fashion." What was all of this? I wanted to scream. She was talking about Kate, in Maryland. I saw her every single time I went to Maryland, and we kept in touch throughout the years. What this woman had just said wasn't true. Stalking someone in uniform? That never happened!

She went on, "He maintained a database on his home computer containing pictures, names, and addresses of approximately 100 women."

There were absolutely no addresses. What I kept on my computer were folders with Facebook pictures of women I knew whose photos I uploaded to DFN. While this certainly is not a particularly cool thing to do, I couldn't figure out why she would lie about me having addresses stored. . Then she accused me of lying about the March 1st issue. She said I told the FBI that I dropped my wife off for lunch on that date, but both my wife and the woman said that they never met on March 1st. The point being that I lied about where I was that day to cover up the fact that I was conducting surveillance.

"This is GPS evidence. He wasn't just in the area. He was on her very block."

Julia Gatto acknowledged that the allegations were horrifying but that it was all fantasy role-play. She brought up Dungeons and Dragons and tried to make the connection that what I was doing was a version of that, albeit a very twisted one. She didn't get to talk for too long before the judge cut her off. The judge pointed out that there were plenty of real world actions that I was doing that were not just fantasy, and he laid out everything the prosecutor just said.

It was hopeless. Julia had no paperwork at all, so anything I said was worthless. It was so frustrating and scary to sit there and listen to that prosecutor spew out a whole bunch of nonsense while I sat there helpless.

At this point, the judge said, "In my twenty years as a prosecutor and a judge, I have never seen allegations as horrifying as these." The thing is, this is probably true, mostly because the allegations were based on a fantasy that literally could never have happened.

As my attorney predicted, I was denied bail. Before I was walked out, Julia said she was going to come visit me later that night. I tried to look for my family again, but I didn't see them.

I was in total shock when I was brought back to the prison. I couldn't believe what was happening. I could not have dreamed up a scenario as devastating as this. When one thinks about it, Kafka could not have dreamed up this scenario. I wanted to scream, and I wanted to cry, but I held it in. This was not how this was supposed to go. Some part of me, a big part of me, thought that when I went to court that it would be over, or at least on the way to being over. Now things were immeasurably worse.

I kept replaying in my mind everything that was said by the prosecutor, and got to work trying to figure it all out. Virtually nothing they said as far as real world acts was true. I had to figure out how to fight all of this.

At one point, I was notified that my attorney was there for a visit. They walked me to one of the rooms for prisoners and lawyers, and for the first time in front of Julia and Alex, her paralegal, who I was meeting for the first time, I broke down uncontrollably.

"Yeah, I know Gil," Julia said sympathetically.

It was hard for me to get any words out for a few minutes. I was just freaking out and crying in front of these two women. I told her that a lot of what the prosecutor said wasn't true. She had a few questions about that, and I gave her what I could, but I was a wreck. I asked about my family. Alex told me that they said they loved me and they don't care what is being said. They don't believe a word of any of it. That made me cry again, and then I asked about Kathleen. She wasn't answering Julia's phone calls.

Somehow Julia was able to calm me down. She told me that they were going to come back tomorrow and they were going to go over the bail hearing step by step. The plan was that I would tell her the truth about my relationship with Kate to start off with. I sensed that Julia believed me but at the same point in her mind she had to believe that these prosecutors had some of this real hard evidence on me. How would I be in this situation otherwise? I had to have done something, right?

Julia explained the discovery process and that the prosecutors would have to turn over every piece of evidence they had. Once my defense had all of that, they would be able to combat it better. For now, Julia said, hang in there, and stay strong.

Despite my professional knowledge of these situations, I still couldn't believe what was happening and I asked her to confirm that being denied bail meant that I had to stay in prison until the trial started.

She sadly nodded yes, but she repeated what she said earlier. "We'll keep applying for bail, and eventually we might have a chance at getting it."

Julia and Alex left, and I was brought back up to my solitary confinement cell where I cried some more. I wondered what my family was doing and how they were handling it. I thought about Kathleen, the baby, my parents, my brothers, and Dudley. I was a total wreck. Later that night, my cellblock got flooded. One of the prisoners was pissed off, stuffed rolls of toilet paper into the toilet and kept flushing until the damn thing overflowed. The water began flowing into my room, and in about an hour it was about a foot deep. I honestly didn't give a shit. I was alone with my thoughts, worried about the case.

I had nothing. Nothing to read, nothing to listen to, no one to talk to. Everything was gone.

"....faces life in prison."

That thought terrified me to no end.

7.

I barely slept that night after the bail hearing. Everything was so bizarre. It seemed like at any moment someone would open up the door to my cell and tell me that they had made a big mistake and let me go. I couldn't stop thinking about Kathleen and my family. At one point, just before the bail hearing began, Julia started to say something about Kathleen, and that newspapers were reporting that she was involved in my arrest somehow, but then the bail hearing started. To say that I was very worried about how she was handling all of this was a huge understatement. I had to let her know that these allegations against me weren't true, and that everything was going to work itself out, but I had no way to talk to her. I felt like I was going insane.

I had no way to talk to my family either. It broke my heart to imagine them at the bail hearing listening to all of the lies about how I was stalking women, even to the point I was supposedly on one woman's block. But that was not the worst part. My family sat there and listened as it was alleged that I was going to kidnap, rape, torture, and cannibalize women. I could not imagine what they were thinking right now.

Of course, I could not stop thinking about my case. I knew I was innocent, but it was becoming clearer to me, all the time, that this was going to be a fight. At least, I had Julia. Although I didn't really know her yet, watching her argue during that first bail hearing, with as much passion as she did, gave me some hope.

Those first days, I had nothing at all to do except sit around stressed out, losing my mind. The anxiety and pain that I felt was overwhelming. I slept fitfully and I rarely ate. The guards gave me my meal trays through a slot in the door, but I barely touched the food. After a couple of days, one of the guards told me that if I continued to refuse to eat, they could force-feed me. I began to flush the food down the toilet. I didn't want any problems with them.

One afternoon, I slept for a few moments and began to dream. I was driving a patrol car with the lights and sirens on, heading to some kind of emergency. When I woke up, I was back in that cold cell wearing my orange jumpsuit. I broke down hysterically. I hated the fact that I woke up from that dream. This would continue to happen a lot more over my time in prison, I'd wake up from a vivid dream about being happy with Kathleen and my daughter, or something work-related, and I'd find myself back in reality. It was always incredibly difficult.

Julia told me that she was going to see me that Friday, which was three days after I was arrested. She said that she was going to come so I could have a little human interaction. I was by myself with nobody to talk to for two full days, with the horrible thoughts, which continually rolled through my mind, as my only companions. I was really looking forward to seeing her. When the day came, I waited anxiously all morning, as I had no idea when she was going to come. Then afternoon came and she still had not arrived. Finally, I began to see the daylight dissipate through the bars in my window. It was almost night time, and she still had not come. I asked one of the guards if I could call my lawyer.

"Do you have a PAC number?" he asked.

I had no idea what that was and I told him that I didn't have one. He said I couldn't make phone calls until I had a PAC number set up. Of course, I asked him how I would get one of those. He told me that I had to wait until the counselor made her rounds and when she did she could set me up with the paperwork. I learned later on that I didn't need a PAC number to call my lawyer. Legal calls were supposed to be free and available when requested. But while I was in solitary confinement for seven months, I was only able to make a grand total of one legal phone call out of approximately fifty requests. The guards were either "too busy", didn't care, or just passed the buck to someone else. It seemed that no one in that building had the authority to grant me a legal phone call while I was in solitary confinement.

Julia never showed up that day or evening. I was absolutely crushed. I was somewhere I should not have been, for a crime I did not commit, and it seemed that nobody cared at all. I wanted to start pounding the door and scream, but, somehow, I kept my cool. All I could do was lay in bed or pace around the filthy, cold, six by eight foot prison cell.

That first weekend was extremely difficult. The ruminating thoughts about my family and Kathleen persisted. I was constantly worrying about them and what they were thinking about all of this. I could not imagine the worry they were feeling, and the humiliation they were going through. I didn't want to be a burden to any of the guards, but the next time one of the officers made a round, I was at my door and asked her, if it wasn't too much trouble, could I please have a pen and some paper?

"Of course, Valle. If you ever need anything, don't worry

about asking us."

She said it in such a nice, pleasant manner, and came right back with a pen and paper. The fact that she was a guard, and even more so that she was a woman and still treated me so kindly, despite the charges against me, meant a lot to me at the time.

I sat down in my cell and wrote a letter to my Mom. She had always been strong and I knew that, out of everyone, she would help me get things done. I started the letter out stating definitively that everything that prosecutor said in court was not true, and that there was an innocent explanation for everything. I told her that I was happy with Julia as my attorney, and that she and everyone else in my life should help Julia with whatever she and her team needed. I told her not to be mad at Kathleen, and that she was probably just as confused as everyone else was about what was going on. I wrote to my mother that someone had to pay the rent for our apartment so that Kathleen still had her home, Kathleen was not working and she and the baby were going to need a place to stay when they came home. I was worried about all of my bills and making sure they were paid. The outside world wasn't going to stop because I was in prison.

I asked another guard for an envelope. I addressed it to my Mom and sealed it. I stuck the envelope in the door feeling that I had finally accomplished something. At least my family would know that all things considered, I was in a good state mentally and that everything would work itself out. I just needed their help to handle things on the outside.

About an hour later, another female guard knocked on my door. She wasn't as friendly as the one who gave me the pen and paper. She told me through the door that I wasn't allowed to seal the envelopes because the guards had to read the letter before it went out. Then she asked me where the stamp for the envelope was.

I told her I didn't have any stamps, she asked me if I had anything in my commissary account. PAC numbers, commissary accounts, I was completely lost on how things worked in prison. She gave me my letter back and said that it couldn't be mailed until I ordered stamps from the commissary. Once again, I was just crushed.

After a brutal weekend, Monday finally came around. I was hoping that Julia would show up, I had been here for six days now and knew nothing about what was going on with the case. She didn't come. Tuesday came and went. No news, no Julia. It wasn't until Wednesday that I found out that New York City had been slammed by Hurricane Sandy three days before. When I asked a guard if I could call my lawyer, he told me that all of the courts were closed, and then he looked at me kind of funny.

"Do you know what's going on out there? It's like *The Walking Dead*."

He told me about the hurricane and all of the devastation it had caused. Sandy had hit New York hard, and I had had no idea. Now I had something else to worry about. Was my family even okay? Were they still alive? The hot water hadn't worked for a few days and inmates were complaining about it. One of them got pissed off and flooded the whole floor just like the other guy had done the previous week. Into my cell came another deluge of someone's toilet water. I was living a nightmare.

Showers were offered but the water was freezing cold, so I chose not to. I didn't have anything to shave with, no deodorant, nothing. I smelled awful but I didn't care. I was all by myself, and that was apparently going to continue for a while. The prison was on full lock down because of the hurricane, which meant no visitors. At least I knew why Julia wasn't coming, but day-by-day the anxiety worsened.

Friday of that week, I had my first major mental breakdown. It had been nine full days since I had any human contact, nine full days that I was locked in that cell. I hadn't gotten any word on how my family was doing, not just regarding my case but also with regard to the hurricane. When one of the guards made a round in the morning, I met him at the door and I begged him to be able to talk to someone. Anyone, I didn't care.

He told me that the psychology department wasn't available. I broke down right in front of him. I told him I was innocent and I was being falsely accused. I kept saying things like, "Just wait until the trial. You'll see. I am not bullshitting, they made a terrible mistake." I was just unloading on him and rambling. Finally he took pity on me and he offered to take me out of the cell for a little while. I turned around and stuck my hands through the slot in the door so he could cuff me, then he took me out and put me in another caged area that said "Recreation." It was bigger than my cell, but was nothing more than an open space where I could walk around. It wasn't much, but it helped a little just to have any sort of a change of scenery.

A few minutes later, a Reverend came walking towards me with the guard who had taken me out of the cell. They met me on the other side of the bars, the guard introduced us, and I thanked them both. The Reverend let me vent for a while, and then started telling me things about how God tests people. While this wasn't particularly helpful to me, at least I had someone to listen to me for a bit. He said a prayer for me, and then he left. The guard came back with another guy, and he introduced him to me as one of the prison psychologists. He pulled up a chair and sat down on the other side of the bars.

"The infamous one!" was the first words out of his mouth.

"Yeah, so I guess you've read about what's going on."

"It's hard to avoid. It's been all over the news."

His whole vibe was really snide and superior, but at least he was someone else to talk to. I started telling him that what they were saying wasn't true and that I was going to be acquitted.

He responded, "Okay, and what makes you think that you are going to beat the federal government at trial?"

To me, it seemed obvious that he couldn't care less about what was going on with me. This guy was supposed to be there for the inmates' mental health? Nevertheless, I talked to him about my side of the story. The thing I was perseverating about most at the moment was what the prosecutors and the feds were saying about my trip to Maryland, and that Kate told the FBI that it was really weird that I suddenly wanted to come down and see her after ten years of very minimal contact between us. I told him there was no way she said that and that it wasn't true. She might be scared and frightened, but there was not a chance in the world that Kate would lie about our friendship like that.

I went on about this for a bit and then he yawned. I told him I was feeling better. I would rather be alone than deal with him. On the way back to my cell, the guard asked me if I wanted something to read. I told him I wasn't sure I could concentrate.

"Right now, you've got nothing but time. You might as well try."

He walked me over to a book cart and I picked out "Angelology" by Danielle Trussing. It was a book on mythology that I thought I might like. When he put me back in the cell and shut the door, he gave me some advice.

"One thing I like to tell people here is, don't worry about the outside. The only thing you can control is how you get through each day. Right now, you can't control anything out there, so it doesn't make sense to worry about it."

He was right. That was better than anything the reverend or the psychologist said. I lay down in bed and started to read the book. I had another long weekend ahead of me.

Sometime around the middle of the following week, things were back to normal at the prison and I heard the words I had been longing to hear for a while.

"Valle! Legal visit!"

Thank God. A couple of days before that, I was hooked up with some soap and deodorant and I was finally able to take a shower. I hadn't shaved though, so I had a rough looking beard going. They handcuffed me and walked me out of my cell and walked me upstairs and put me in a room with a glass partition in the middle and uncuffed me. Then Alex, the paralegal, was brought in on the other side of the partition. It was so good to see her.

The first thing she told me was that everyone in my family was fine from the hurricane, and that they were all worried about how I was doing. She also told me again that they didn't care what was being said and written about me, and that they knew I was innocent. They wanted me to be strong, be truthful, and defend myself. We didn't get too much into the case. I asked her if there was a lot about this in the media, and what kinds of things were being put out there. She hesitated and said that there was a lot of stupid stuff being written, but that not everything was completely negative. She mentioned a column from the New York Post that brought up the fact that I didn't really do anything.

She asked me how I was doing. I told her that I was freaking out about my rent, my bills, Kathleen, and the baby. Every day, I was becoming more and more worried about what was going on with Kathleen. Alex said that she didn't have any more information on Kathleen and whether or not she was actually involved in any of this.

Before she left, Alex said that Julia was going to come back the next day. They were working on getting another bail hearing and she told me that a lot of really smart people are working hard on my behalf, and that everyone felt that it was going to work out. For the first time in a long time, I went back to my cell feeling good. My family was okay, and they were staying strong. Julia was going to come the next day and we were going to start on our defense.

As promised, she showed up with Alex the next morning. "Gil, this is a bullshit fucking case! It really is a bullshit fucking case!" Julia said.

She told me that we had another bail hearing set for the next day and that it was going to be done in a way that hopefully the press wouldn't know about it. She thought we would have a better chance in an empty courtroom without the media present. She said that the hurricane took my case out of the limelight. Hopefully, that was going to be to our advantage, as people had a chance to step away from the horrible allegations and think about something else. She brought up the fact that I was supposedly on a woman's block stalking her, and I told her again, definitively, that one day I did drop Kathleen off for lunch in that area, but there had to be something else. She asked me about patrol, and if I was ever allowed to be out on an assignment out of my precinct.

That rung a bell. CRV: Critical Response Vehicle. It was an anti-terrorism deployment that involved two cops in one patrol car from every precinct in the city meeting in Manhattan, and then getting assigned to a post at what might be a potential terrorist target. We were posted at landmarks and hotels mostly, but also synagogues, churches, and mosques. When the Batman shooting happened in Colorado, cops were posted at movie theaters all over the city. I talked, while Julia and Alex wrote furiously.

At the time, I was assigned as my sergeant's driver. When we were assigned to CRV, it was my sergeant's responsibility to make sure that the cops on her roster were all on their posts, so for me it was basically like a day off. I drove her from post to post, and the rest of the day, we would just patrol. The entire borough of Manhattan was essentially our beat. Julia seemed rejuvenated. She was convinced that there had to be an innocent explanation for everything that they claimed. My cell phone pinging off of a tower, somewhere in Manhattan, during one of these CRV assignments, was far more likely to be what happened, as opposed to me sitting on a woman's block conducting surveillance so I could kidnap her, murder her, and then eat her.

That was the big piece of "evidence" that we were going to refute at the next day's hearing. We still did not have any discovery paperwork turned over from the prosecutors. Julia was optimistic that we'd make bail. For the first time since I had been put in jail, I had hope. Maybe I could go home tomorrow, I could talk to my family, and maybe even to Kathleen.

I was taken out of my cell early the next morning and brought to court. I still hadn't shaved, and still hadn't seen or spoken with my family. I sat, very nervous and anxious, in a cell in the courthouse. I didn't think I would be able to handle being denied bail and being brought back up to that frigid and filthy cell. The bail package we were proposing was as strict as it gets. Home confinement, strict pre-trial monitoring, a bond signed by about 6 different people, surrendering my passport, no computer usage, it went on and on. I didn't care. I just wanted out of there.

Two marshals unlocked the cell door and walked me down the hall towards the courtroom. I entered through a side door and looked to the left. The courtroom was mostly empty, but in the second row were my Dad, my Mom, and my two brothers. My father smiled and nodded his head, and my mother gave me thumbs up and mouthed, "Stay strong." I sat next to Julia. The courtroom was set up so that the prosecutors were at a table in front of us. Julia put her arm around me and asked how I was feeling. I was incredibly nervous and, as much as she was trying not to show it, I am sure she was too. Then Julia said that Hadassa Waxman had just asked her how I was holding up and that she had been thinking about me during the storm.

"Are you fucking kidding me?" I asked

Julia was perplexed too. She said that if she cared so much about how I was holding up, then she should stop arguing against our bail package.

The judge entered the courtroom, a different one from the first hearing, and everything got rolling. The judge let Julia speak first. She started off with the "journey."

It was the first time I heard Julia mention the "journey." It became somewhat of our calling card over time. Here was the journey, you hear or read about the allegations against me and you are completely horrified by them. Then you read the complaint again and you start to notice holes. You fully acknowledge that the subject matter is abhorrent and disgusting, but you start to ask yourself, what really happened here? You then find out that actually, nothing happened. This was a fantasy life, completely separate from reality. Nothing in real life actually happened. Julia went on to compare it to Dungeons and Dragons, a popular role-playing game where players take on a different persona and go back and forth with each other about adventures that they are going to go on together. Julia continued, saying that the chats and emails describe a mountain house that doesn't actually exist. Further, the FBI didn't find any ropes, chloroform, or torture tools when they searched my apartment. Most importantly, there was never any attempt to actually kidnap anyone. There were no real world steps taken. This was all a fantasy.

Waxman, of course, refuted that when it became her chance to speak. "Ms. Gatto is leaving out a lot of reality here," she said to the judge, as she began describing the alleged evidence that supposedly placed me on the woman's block. She said that the chats involved detailed plans about women that I knew, and that I was going to use the fact that I knew them to my advantage. Although acknowledging the bail package as onerous, she maintained that I was a flight risk because I was facing life in prison, and also, purportedly, I was a danger to the community. Moreover, she asserted that I would be able to use the phone or the U.S. Mail to communicate with my "co-conspirators."

There she went again. Another lie. The only inference a person could draw from that statement was that I actually knew the people I was role-playing with on the Internet. Saying in court that I was able to call them on the phone, or write them mail was essentially saying that I knew these people in real life. That angered me because they knew that was not the case. I knew nothing about these people, nor how to communicate with them outside of the websites and Yahoo Messenger.

She also claimed that I had files on my home computer that were filled with personal details of around 100 women. Those files, she said, contained photos, names, addresses, and physical descriptions of them. That was another blatant misrepresentation. The "files" she referred to were folders with Facebook pictures that I used in the role-plays. Nothing else.

Despite the prosecutor's attempts at slandering me, the judge seemed to be siding with us. Julia began to address the issue of me being on the woman's block. She went into a description about the CRV assignment, and that the whole borough of Manhattan was my beat, and that it simply could have been me driving around that area and my cell phone pinged off of a cell tower while I was there.

The prosecutor got up and said, "Your Honor, this isn't just in the area. His cell phone puts him on her very block." She went on to talk about the trip to Maryland. Julia responded to this by saying that I went down, along with Kathleen and our baby, spent the weekend there, and saw a lot of people, Kate being one of them, but that there was nothing unusual about it since I was University of Maryland alum and made multiple trips there every year.

The judge still seemed to be siding with us. He told the prosecutor that her case, as of that moment, still left a lot of doubt as to whether or not this was a real conspiracy. He acknowledged the graphic, disgusting nature of the chats, and said that they should make us all be concerned, but without any real world actions, how could it be a real conspiracy? He informed us that he was reserving his decision as to whether or not he was going to grant me bail, and that he would issue a ruling in writing in the coming days.

When the judge left, Julia said, "That went about as well as it could possibly go." I was really proud of her, and I felt some real hope. As I was walked out of the courtroom, I took one more look at my family. They all looked pretty optimistic. The marshals who escorted me back to the prison echoed what Julia said about how well that went. They said that hopefully, I'd be going home tomorrow. A couple of minutes later, however, one of them notified us that the judge wanted us back in court. They didn't know why, but one of them guessed that maybe the judge had a ruling already.

They brought me back in, and Julia told me that one of the "victims" had a lawyer that wanted to speak at the hearing. The judge came back in and was unsure whether or not she was legally allowed to speak at a bail hearing. He said that he was going to check on it and get back to us. I was brought back to my cell for the night. I was feeling good, and for the first time I actually got some decent sleep. It seemed that the tide was starting to turn.

What happened next was bizarre. I only know how everything at the next hearing played out because I was able to read the transcript later on. The Federal Defenders office wrote to the judge and said that they waived any objection to letting the other lawyer speak in the hope that doing that would allow the judge to rule on my bail more quickly. The judge called everyone in for a hearing the next day. Julia was away for a wedding, so I had a lawyer who I hadn't met in the courtroom. There was some mix-up that prevented me from being there at the appointed time. The judge asked where I was and if we wanted the hearing delayed until I was brought to the courtroom, which probably would have taken hours.

My lawyer lied and told the judge that I waived my right to be there. I never waived my right to be there. Had I been there, I have no doubt that things would have played out differently. The "victim's" lawyer got up and spoke about a real world action that was supposedly a step in furtherance of the conspiracy to kidnap her client. She said that I was obsessed with her client, and that I demonstrated my obsession by having a third party deliver a "token" to her as a surprise. She said that her client felt completely creeped out by that and couldn't figure out why I would have a third party deliver that to her, but after learning of the allegations against me it all made sense. This "token," she argued to the judge, was an attempt on my part to try to get closer to her. It was to try to earn her trust, so that, eventually, I could get her alone and kidnap her.

This swayed the judge. He was now fully on board with the prosecutors and since I wasn't there, there was nothing my lawyer could say to refute this claim. Of course, I knew exactly what this lawyer was talking about, and it was completely innocent. But without further information from me, the judge said that this incident "adds some color" to the allegations and that it was a step in the direction to kidnap her. He denied me bail.

While all of this happened, I was in my cell. It was dark out, and I heard a guard yell out: "Valle! Legal visit!"

I was thrilled. I wondered if I was getting some good news. Maybe the judge issued his ruling in writing and I was going to go home soon. When I walked into the room, Alex was the only one there. I was incredibly nervous.

"I have some bad news and some good news."

I already knew what the bad news was before she even had to say it. The judge denied me bail. What else could it be? The good news? He seemed to poke a lot of holes and raised a lot of questions in the prosecution's case that we could use as a target. But I was distraught. How did we lose? The judge seemed to be in our corner.

Alex then got into the issue with the "token" and asked me about it. I was absolutely furious. They were seriously arguing that this was an overt act and the judge bought it? While Alex wrote, I explained everything.

At the beginning of every year, I got twenty Patrolmen's Benevolent Association cards. The PBA is the police union, and cops could give these cards out to friends and family. If someone was pulled over for a traffic violation by a cop and they had a PBA card, it was very likely that the cop would exercise discretion and let the person go with a warning. I always had a handful of extra cards, so I asked Kathleen if she had any friends who she thought might want one. She immediately gave me the name of one of her friends.

"She would be absolutely tickled pink if she got one!" Kathleen said.

She was right. This was the "victim" that was being referred to, and it was one of Kathleen's old teacher friends. I was Facebook friends with her, and on several separate occasions she tagged me in some kind of NYPD related photo. One time, it was an NYPD teddy bear she saw in some store. Another time it was a T-shirt. She had asked me many times if I had any single cop friends. I invited her to one of the precinct's Christmas parties with Kathleen and she had a lot of fun. So she was a girl who Kathleen and I were pretty close with.

I filled the card out with her name, my name, and my cell phone number, which was standard practice. I filled out every card I gave out the same way. I left it with Kathleen and told her to give it to her next time she saw her. Kathleen and I had our baby by now, so the next time she saw this woman wasn't for another few months, which was the time I dropped Kathleen off for lunch with her on my way to work. Kathleen gave her the PBA card, and told me later on that the woman was practically jumping up and down in complete awe of the PBA card.

That was the "token," and Kathleen was the third party. That disgusting, mendacious lawyer spun that whole thing in such a ridiculous way and the judge bought it. Even worse, I had a lawyer there who told the judge that I had waived my right to be there. Because of this, the deceptive story about a third party delivering a token couldn't be refuted, and it had cost me bail.

Distraught and frustrated, I was returned to my cell. Hadassa Waxman was lying about a whole bunch of things, and now this other lawyer had thrown me under the bus, and had done it in such a way that would make the U.S. Attorney's Office proud. We didn't have any of this so-called evidence turned over to us yet, so it was their word against ours. Of course, the "holier-than-thou" U.S. Attorneys would never lie, right? Of course not, they are righteous people, the best of the best. [Sarcasm intended.] Except that I knew they were lying, and I was up against them as well as the seemingly indomitable aura that surrounds them. It was starting to get incredibly scary.

Julia came to see me a couple of days later and we got to work again. I cleared up the story with the token. Then she told me something I'll never forget.

"You see how they twist and spin things? But the perception is that defense lawyers are the ones who are shady and pull tricks."

She was right. As a cop I had held that perception too but what was happening here was an eye-opening experience. We had a judge assigned for the trial now, Paul Gardephe. Julia told me that his reputation is someone that is right down the middle. We could have gotten a better draw, but it also could have been worse. I had another court appearance coming up before Judge Gardephe where I was going to enter my "Not Guilty" plea. That went down nice and easy and was basically a non-event, but in a couple of days we were going to have a bail hearing before him.

"Two judges already denied your client, so you have a long road to hoe," the judge said to Julia.

Julia and I met later that night. Judge Gardephe came off as a bit intimidating, but I knew that Julia was going to give it her best shot. Our plan was to explain the "token" story and talk about how it was twisted in an attempt to create a fictional plot that didn't exist. She had also done some more research on cell towers, but we still had none of this "evidence." If the prosecutor wanted to keep saying that they had evidence that I was on that woman's very block, there wasn't much we could do. Before she left, I asked her something that I had been wondering about for a while now.

"Where is the police department?" I had been a good cop and was expecting, or at least hoping, that they would have my back during this.

Julia told me that they went to the precinct a couple of times, but they were shunned by everyone. They asked to talk to my PBA delegates, but they ignored her as well. That was very disappointing and infuriating. As far as I was concerned, the NYPD was dead to me.

Julia had some good news though. She scheduled a psychological evaluation that we would be able to use as part of the bail hearing. She had no doubt that the report would come back that I was not a danger to people. She also told me that Pretrial Services had changed their mind, and they were going to recommend that I be granted bail. Things were looking up again. I met with a male doctor and his female assistant. The woman tried to act friendly, but it was obvious that she was very uncomfortable in my presence. The doctor asked some detailed questions, and the whole thing lasted about three hours, but it went very well. He wrote a report that said I wasn't a danger to anyone, and Julia forwarded that to the judge prior to the bail hearing.

The prosecutors also forwarded a letter to the judge, and, of course, it was full of more lies. Here were blatant misrepresentations of facts, in writing. To me, this was even worse because they couldn't be defended as a slip of the tongue during an oral argument. The letter said that they had done some forensic testing on my computer and the results showed that I had files on eighty something women, with their names, addresses, and physical descriptions. That wasn't true. They also said that while I was chatting with MoodyBlues, I sent him over a document that was a blueprint outlining a plan to kidnap Kate from Maryland. Though there was a document, it was full of fictional information and was just a prop that I used in the role-play. True to form, they lied in the letter and said that I provided him with Kate's real personal information. Even worse, they said they discovered that I had provided true and accurate personal information of every single woman I had role-played about with my chat partners. They said, "Every piece of personal information sent by Valle, we found to be true and accurate." Lie after lie after lie.

The bail hearing was late the next day. The courtroom was packed again, like it had been for that first appearance. I was able to see that my family was there. I sat next to Julia and took a deep breath. This was it.

Julia spoke first. She began again with the "journey," and then got into the fact that it was all fantasy role-play, and that there were no real world acts that I had ever committed, let alone any crimes. Judge Gardephe interrupted her and asked about the trip to Maryland. I was glad that the judge seemed engaged in talking everything through. Julia explained the trip perfectly, then went on to elaborate and stressed the fact that nothing was found in my apartment during the search. It was all fantasy. It was all storytelling that took place on the Internet. Further, she chastised the other lawyer who told the token story. She said that the government is cherry picking innocent everyday interactions and spinning them to make them look creepy and suspicious.

Waxman then stood up and said a lot of the same nonsense as she had before. She said, yet again, that the FBI had GPS evidence that I was on that woman's block. She hammered me and called me a danger to the community and a flight risk, and that there was no conceivable way I could be granted bail. She then said that they discovered a new incident where I conducted surveillance. It was in August, and it was around ground zero in lower Manhattan. According to her, my phone pinged off of a tower down there around some other woman's office building, and they checked my work records which showed that I wasn't assigned to CRV, or any other assignment that had me in lower Manhattan.

Since I was there this time, I was able to fight this one. I remembered exactly what happened. My friend from Maryland came up and spent the weekend with us. We went to a Yankee game on Saturday, and then on Sunday I showed him around lower Manhattan and we walked by ground zero. Of course my work records showed that I wasn't assigned to lower Manhattan, because I was off from work that day.

As usual, I wanted to scream but I had to sit there, listen to the lies, and stay silent. It was an utterly helpless feeling. There was nothing we could do. Julia did the best that she could and explained the August incident, pointing out that, not only was I off from work, but it wouldn't make sense for me to be conducting surveillance at an office building where a woman works on a day that she was off. But apparently, Judge Gardephe had his mind made up before the bail hearing even started. He read from a detailed statement that he had written before the hearing even started.

What angered me the most is that in denying me bail, he cited each of Waxman's lies, including what had just been sent to him in her letter, which said that every piece of personal information I sent was true and including the new "surveillance" incident, which we had just explained. He disregarded the doctor's report, which confirmed that I had no homicidal tendencies, and said that it is clear from the evidence thus far that I do have homicidal thoughts, and that it appeared I had taken active steps to bring these horrible plans to fruition. He went on and on, and said that the fact that I appeared to have a normal life, newly married with a baby, made this even more frightening because it seemed that I had gone undetected while planning out kidnapping and cannibalism murders. As he was reading, I saw Waxman turn her head to the right. She had a smug look on her face that I will never forget.

It was clear to me that Judge Gardephe hated me. I was facing an uphill battle against the U.S. Attorney's office, which was demonstrating itself as an Augean stable, and a judge who detested me. Nobody knew the truth yet. Not even Julia. I am sure she believed everything I was telling her, but none of this evidence they said they had was turned over, so all she had was my word.

When I was led out of court, I took one more look at my family. My dad was crushed. My mom shook her head and yelled forcefully, "Stay strong!" It was November 20th. I would not see them again until the middle of February, a week before the trial.

The next day in prison, there was a newspaper circling around. Sometimes the guards would pass them around so the inmates could read them. The New York Times from November 21st was in my hands. Of course, there was an article about me. The one line I remember was, "The case has been seen as one of the most disturbing and unusual involving a New York City Police Officer."

It was tough to read. The guy in the cell next to me knocked on my wall and asked me if I saw the article. We had gotten to talking a bit before that day through the wall. He had a thick southern accent and he was known as "Tennessee." We talked sports here and there, but he hadn't mentioned my case until he asked me about the article. I told him that I saw it.

"There ain't no crime there from everything I read," he said to me. That made me feel better. I had someone other than my family and my lawyers on my side. He went on to say that everyone on the cellblock knew who I was, and everyone agreed that the case was complete nonsense. He told me to stay strong, man up, and I'll get through this. Even though I never even saw his face, it still made me feel good to know someone was on my side.

Julia came to visit me the next day and we got to work. The first words out of her mouth were, "Gil, we cannot lose."

She looked me right in the eyes and said again, "We cannot lose, because that man would be the one sentencing you."

She was talking about Judge Gardephe who just gave me the worst verbal beat down I had ever heard in denying me bail. Julia was absolutely right. We could not lose. If we did, I would be spending the rest of my life in prison.

8.

December 14, 2012, was one of the roughest days I had in solitary confinement. A couple of weeks before that, one of the guards slipped me a radio and some headphones to help me pass the time. That was such a nice gesture that I will never forget it.

Since I had the radio, I was able to hear about the events that unfolded in Newtown, Connecticut, at Sandy Hook Elementary School, on the morning of December 14th. The slaughter that took place at that elementary school rocked me to my core. When my duties as a cop brought me to a tragedy, I would go home later that night and want to hug Kathleen and my daughter and not let go. On December 14th, my 51st day in solitary confinement, I had nobody.

"Hadassa Waxman belongs in jail! She belongs in fucking jail!"

It was a few days later, in mid-December, and Julia was visiting me in prison. She was angry. It was obvious how upset she was, she had fire in her eyes. When all of my chances at bail were exhausted, the prosecutors started turning over some of their so-called evidence to us. This meant either Julia or someone else from the Federal Defenders office was at the prison around four times a week so that we could start to seriously prepare for trial. We had a trial date set for late January, which was extremely soon, but I wanted that because I was innocent and I was in solitary confinement. I didn't see any reason to prolong my misery any longer.

My federal defenders were on board with that, but they acknowledged that it would be very tough to pull everything together by then. The prosecutors wanted to push the trial back but Judge Gardephe denied their request.

A large portion of the voluminous paperwork that was turned over to us was records of my chats and e-mails. I already knew this was the case, but this made it very clear to everyone else that I never provided true personal information about the women I was role-playing with the people I was chatting with. That flew in the face of Waxman's repeated claims in court that every piece of personal information I sent over the Internet was true and accurate. They also turned over all of the FBI's interview notes of each woman they interviewed. They had interviewed people I hadn't seen since I was six years old; it was amazing the desperation they were showing to try to convict me. The one that stuck out though was the interview they conducted with Kate.

The interview was done seven weeks prior to the last bail hearing on November 20th, so the prosecutors knew exactly what was said by Kate to the FBI. On November 20th, Hadassa Waxman told Judge Gardephe that Kate thought it was weird of me to try to schedule brunch with her because she had not seen me in such a long time, and that we had been in minimal contact for six years since we graduated from Maryland. The interview notes, however, revealed that Kate told the FBI that she considered me a good friend and that we would get together whenever I was in Maryland. We got together four or five times a year, every year, since we graduated from college. That was what she really told the FBI, and that information was documented and given to Waxman before the first bail hearing.

That was what set Julia off more than anything. It was

clear that this was not a level playing field. Julia said that if a defense attorney lied in court like that, they could be suspended or disbarred, but prosecutors can say virtually anything they want, and they are rarely held accountable. I began to see a new confidence in Julia around the case. She now realized that everything I was saying was true. I think she knew it was true even before, but now she had proof that anyone could see. Some of her associates at the Federal Defenders office were deep in research about cell phone tower science. To this point, the FBI had not said what kind of evidence they had that led Waxman to definitively say that I was on a woman's block, but we were going to be prepared.

Our thought was that they were relying on my phone signal pinging off a cell tower that was on that particular woman's block, but anyone in law enforcement knows that this is no way to pinpoint a specific location. This only showed that my phone was within a certain radius. That particular cell tower, my defense team found, had a radius of 500 yards. Something else that was turned over as part of their paper dump was my work records. They showed that on the day in question, I was assigned to the CRV anti-terrorism assignment and I was driving the sergeant as I had theorized before. I definitely had an innocent reason for being within 500 yards of a building on the Upper East Side of Manhattan.

Not only that, but depending on cell traffic, cell phones don't always ping off of the nearest tower. Someone on my defense team found a great example of this. On December 4, 2011, at 10:35 p.m., my cell phone pinged off of a tower in Edgewater, New Jersey, which is across the Hudson River. At 10:36, my phone hit off of a tower on another building in Edgewater. Under the FBI's theory, that would place me somewhere in the vicinity of Edgewater, New Jersey, but my work records showed that I was assigned to patrol in my precinct that day and that I responded to a 911 call at 10:45 p.m. in Harlem, ten minutes after my cell phone supposedly placed me in New Jersey.

All of this was very good for my case. I was so impressed and proud of the representation I was getting from public defenders, and I loved that Julia was yelling that Hadassa Waxman belonged in prison. I had no doubt that these people were working incredibly hard for me and each day I was getting more and more optimistic about my chances. I knew I was innocent, now I knew we could prove it.

Since my lawyers were at the prison nearly every day, I wasn't spending as much time in my cell and when I was there, I was poring over paperwork. The chats and e-mails were very hard to read. When I wrote all of this stuff I was hiding behind an anonymous screen name trying to sound as graphic and detailed as possible, because that was all a part of the fantasy. It was supposed to be dark, weird, and sexual because it was all a game played by strangers on the Internet. Now, it was Gil Valle who had written all of this, and it was going to be their main evidence at trial. I didn't know how to mentally prepare for that embarrassment. I would go over and over the trial in my head. Who was going to be there? Who was going to testify? How much press would it get? Still, things were looking good. Their main two pieces of real world evidence - the cell phone tower and the trip to Maryland - were going to be refuted by my work records, science, and Kate's own statement to the FBI.

As this was all going on I found out for sure that Kathleen was the one who got this all rolling when she reached out to the FBI. I guess I always suspected that, even at the beginning, but I didn't want to think about it. This information also showed that Foto lied to me when he said that they had been monitoring me for a year and a half.

It wasn't that I ever blamed Kathleen for going to the authorities. I still don't, to this day. I knew that her first thought when she found everything was that she wasn't giving up on us, and we were going to find a couples' therapist and work this out. I do, however, acknowledge the complete shock she must have felt. At some point, over the following days when she was home in Nevada, she decided to contact law enforcement. Maybe she was talked into it, I don't know. But I sincerely believe that she was hoping the FBI would come back to her and say that this was nothing and that she was safe. It was just fantasy after all, she had nothing to worry about. This is what a competent law enforcement agent would say. Instead, the case ended up in the hands of a rookie agent who didn't even know how to interpret cell towers. Instead of being placed in the hands of professionals who could advise her on the difference between fantasy and reality, she was goaded into hysteria.

Through the documents produced in response to our discovery, I found out that the FBI had placed a tracker on my cell phone for thirty days. They indicated in their paperwork that they were expecting me to lead them to further evidence of the kidnapping conspiracy, namely the mountain house in the middle of nowhere.

Of course, none of that existed so what they saw while tracking me for thirty days was a man who went to and from work and occasionally took his dog for a walk at the park. Since I was so depressed after Kathleen left, I wasn't in the mood to socialize with anyone very much. Sometimes when I was in my cell thinking about the case, I would start to laugh out loud when I imagined Agent Foto, Agent Warden, and every other person involved in this case looking for the mountain house, torture tools, a white van, and everything else that I had mentioned in my fantasy world. I would literally laugh out loud, and not be able to stop for five or ten minutes. I had been in solitary confinement for about two months, and I still had not been able to see or speak to my family. Julia and the rest of the federal defenders were my pipeline to everyone in the outside world. At times, I thought I was going crazy.

Even though we were gaining some momentum, Christmas was a very dark day. I tried not to think about it, so I listened to the radio, but Christmas was being mentioned on every station I listened to. When I turned the radio off, I thought about my family and my daughter. I wondered if Kathleen had taken her to see Santa Claus. I remembered that Kathleen and I talked about how we were going to put a Santa hat on Dudley. I closed my eyes and tried to imagine that moment. I imagined the sounds of my wife and daughter laughing. I just wanted to picture it for a minute. I would give anything to take my mind out of there and imagine that moment for just one minute. It was a moment I would sell my soul to the devil to have. I felt a tear rolling down my cheek, then I opened my eyes again and I was back in the reality of solitary confinement, back in the six by eight foot cell. I had been alone now for sixty-one days. I tried to tell myself that next Christmas would be different.

After that rough day, Julia had more good news. Dr. Park Dietz, a world-renowned forensic psychologist and criminologist who lives in California, was going to fly across the country and interview me for the case. His résumé was impressive, and most of the time, he testified for the prosecution. He provided expert opinion or testimony in the cases of John Hinckley (the guy who tried to kill Ronald Reagan), Jeffrey Dahmer (an actual cannibal), the D.C. snipers, the Unabomber, and many others.

I was thrilled that a guy with a big name and a good reputation was going to interview me. I knew that I would never hurt anybody so I had nothing to hide. I thought this could be a game changer for me. The tide was finally turning. We had proof now that the prosecutors were lying, the federal defenders worked hard every day, and now Dr. Dietz was on board. I was really looking forward to going to trial so that I could clear my name.

Dr. Dietz's evaluation took place over three full days, December 31st to January 2nd from eight in the morning until around five p.m. He left his wife and family and spent the New Year in New York City, in a prison, so that he could do the interview. I was so grateful for that. He said that he was aware that we had a very tight window and that the trial was coming up, so he felt he owed it to me. The three days were mentally exhausting. After each day, I went back to my cell and went right to sleep. Those three nights were the best sleep I had gotten during the whole twenty-one months, because I was so mentally spent.

I felt really nervous on the first day because I still had never completely explained how I wound up on the Dark Fetish Network to anyone. This would be the very first time in my life I would talk openly and in depth to anyone about my inner sexual desires.

He put me at ease when he told me he had heard literally everything under the sun, and that my sexual fetishes were actually not unusual. He just told me to be completely forthright and honest about everything, and I was. We turned over every stone from my early childhood with my parents getting divorced, to puberty and the realization that I was aroused by images of women in bondage, to my relationships with women in high school and college, my years with the NYPD, and my participation on the Dark Fetish Network. Similar to my post-arrest interview with the FBI, we went over my relationships with the women who the government was labeling as victims. All of that took three days and when that was over, I took a couple of written tests.

Of course, I passed everything and Dr. Dietz concluded that I am the furthest thing from a homicidal maniac. He would later write, "It is my professional opinion that Mr. Valle has been sexually stimulated by images and thoughts of other men abducting and binding females since he was a teenager, without ever attempting to abduct or bind a female in any manner whatsoever. Mr. Valle came to have erotic fantasies in which he imagined other men using chloroform to abduct women, whom they would hogtie, oil, and truss up in preparation for cooking. Despite the various fantasies, I found no evidence whatsoever that Mr. Valle ever harmed, or actually intended to harm, any woman."

"Despite government assertions that Mr. Valle was, in effect, on the verge of acting to implement his thoughts through conduct, literally every tidbit of evidence argued by the government in support of Valle's guilt is equally consistent with Valle being among the great many men with similar patterns of sexual arousal who do not commit crimes, rather than being among the far smaller number of men with similar patterns of sexual arousal who do commit violent crimes. Not a single fact put forth by the government is more probative of planning and intent than of fantasy, sharing fantasies, and fiction writing. And those who enjoy writing and collaborating on what they find to be erotic stories, as Mr. Valle did, also research their topics for stimulation or to add realism to their fantasies and stories. For Mr. Valle and his collaborators, the conversations are appreciated precisely because they mimic reality; the more realistic the conversations seem, the greater the arousal and appreciation."

"The use of imagined or photographic images of 'real' women in erotic fantasies is universal, whether or not the women have offered up their images for such use and the fact that Mr. Valle built erotic fantasies around women he knew does not make him the least bit unusual. Without any consent whatsoever, normal men incorporate images of women they've noticed into their erotic fantasies during sex, masturbation, and passing thoughts."

"I believe Mr. Valle was communicating over the Internet, through such websites as darkfetishnet.com and with anonymous strangers he met thereon, simply as a means of coping with the fact that he was aroused by socially unacceptable images and fantasies. Mr. Valle achieved acceptance from others, encouragement for his writings (some aspects of which were designed to arouse others and generate approval, as they did not appeal to him), and at times, sexual stimulation. But for Mr. Valle, the character was a role only, an exercise in sexual imagination and collaborative creative writing."

"There is no evidence that Mr. Valle assembled a kidnap and rape kit, accessed a suitable vehicle, or accessed an isolated or soundproof location. There is no evidence that Mr. Valle ever committed any abortive attempts to commit an abduction, rape, torture, or homicide. Thus, in my opinion, there is no reliable evidence to suggest that his erotic conversations could reasonably be construed as conspiratorial plans rather than conversations that were an end in themselves."

"Mr. Valle's Internet communications and related behavior (e.g., engaging in online research about kidnapping women and posting pictures of women he knew) are fully consistent with non-criminal activities designed to stimulate and entertain himself, his readers, and his collaborators with erotic fantasies, pornography, erotic stories, and erotic role-play."

Reading this now, it may seem to you to be common sense. Of course, men fantasize about women without their consent; it is just that my fantasies are a bit different. But in this Kafkaesque circus of a criminal case, it needed to be explained to the judge and the jury, and now I had one of the foremost experts in the nation testifying on my behalf. I was getting more and more optimistic.

After the New Year, Julia was at the prison every day, including weekends. Julia is an attractive, funny, feisty and no-nonsense kind of woman, but it was apparent the stress was taking its toll. She had the life of an innocent man in her hands. She was having trouble sleeping and had bags under her eyes that were out of this world. On top of my case, she and her family were also in the process of moving. I can't imagine what life was like for her during this time.

We were informed that the government added a new attorney to the case, a guy named Randall Jackson. Julia said that this guy basically just screams and yells for dramatic effect, so my thought was that he was just brought on to try and scare the jury and browbeat them into thinking that I was a terrifying maniac.

There were a couple of pre-trial hearings and now even Judge Gardephe seemed to be starting to get it. He berated the prosecutors for not submitting something on a timely basis, and he questioned them about the cell phone evidence that they claimed placed me "on the very block." They were changing their tune a bit, and now the phrase was "in the vicinity." We were trying to have this evidence precluded from the trial because it was inconclusive and could be misleading to the jury.

"When you say 'in the vicinity,' could you give me a sense of what you mean by that?" Judge Gardephe asked Randall Jackson during a pre-trial conference.

"Your Honor, I think that our witness, taking a look at the data and applying it to the maps, would say that it's probably four or five blocks," Randall Jackson responded.

I sat there and just shook my head. For three months, they were saying in court that this evidence didn't just place me in the area, but on the very block. Now, it was four or five blocks. It got even better a week later when the government submitted a brief indicating that their witness would testify that I was within five hundred to six hundred yards of the cell tower. That's five or six football fields. Anyone who is familiar with how the blocks of Manhattan are structured knows that I could have been blocks and blocks away. Better still, the records turned over by the government showed that the phone call I made that day that put me in that area was made to Kathleen, not some non existent "co-conspirator".

About ten days before trial, Julia and I spent all of our time together preparing for my testimony. I was going to have to talk about masturbation, my kinked out fantasies, and all other kinds of embarrassing things in front of a packed courtroom. I wouldn't wish that on my worst enemy, but it had to be done. The U.S. Attorney's office was going to portray me a certain way, and the jury had to see and hear me for themselves.

While we were talking, I made an intelligent point about something. I don't remember what it was, but Julia was impressed.

"You're really smart, you know that? You'll be all right once this is all over. There might be some opportunities for you, but you're going to be okay," she said.

"Yeah, look where being smart got me," I replied.

"Yeah, because you are so fucking stupid! You are seriously so fucking stupid Gil!"

Despite the stress we both felt, Julia and I were able to occasionally laugh with an exchange like that. She was becoming less of a lawyer, and more of a friend.

The trial was going to start the following Monday. The Wednesday before, we wrapped up for the day. Before she left, Julia told me that the day before one of the prison guards told her that she has to win this case for me.

"There isn't an ounce of evil in that man's body," the female guard had told her.

Julia also said one more thing before she left that night.

"We're going to win."

At six a.m. the next morning, Thursday, one of the guards knocked on my door and woke me up.

"Pack up," he said.

I asked him what was going on and he said he had no idea. He told me to just pack all of my stuff. I didn't have much other than legal paperwork, but I got it all ready and waited. I was thinking they might have dropped the case. Am I going home? Is it possible? My mind and my heart were racing. A few minutes later, two guards came back and took me out of the cell. They brought me downstairs and handed me the dark blue outfit that prisoners would wear to court. No one told me what was going on, but I had the sense they didn't know either.

I ended up in a small cell somewhere in the courthouse. The marshals kept me isolated from other prisoners because I was a police officer. The cell was so small that I couldn't even lie down on a bench. There were no windows and I had no sense of time, but my body clock was telling me that an hour passed, then two, then three. I was still in there, and no one checked on me or told me what was happening. I was tired of pacing around, so I lay down on the freezing cold floor. Hours and hours went by, and still nothing. The possibility of something good happening left my mind, and I had no doubt now what was going on.

The U.S. Attorney's office was screwing with me.

Much later that night, still having no clue what time it was, I was pulled out of the cell. My wrists and ankles were shackled, and I was told that I was being transferred to another facility. They walked me to a bus and, in the process, I had my first whiff of fresh air in over three months. It was late January, it was dark out and it was freezing. I boarded a bus that was full of other inmates and didn't say a word to anyone. We arrived at the Metropolitan Detention Center, a federal detention center in Brooklyn. I was tired, stressed out, and extremely pissed off. I kept wondering if Julia, or if anyone else, knew what was going on. I had missed an entire day of trial prep with her.

They walked me into the building and put me into another cell. I could see a clock on a wall in the distance. It was a little after ten p.m. I sat in that cell until 3:15 in the morning, and then I was pulled out and brought upstairs into a solitary confinement cell with nothing in it but a toilet and a bed. There was no window. I lay in bed, unable to sleep, and continued to wonder what the hell was going on. I was legitimately scared. A couple of hours later, a guard pounded on my door.

"Valle! Get ready for court!"

I was ready. I didn't take my jumper off and I didn't have any of my belongings back. I couldn't brush my teeth, shave, or shower. I was brought back downstairs and put in the same cell that I was in about 3 hours earlier. I was put on another bus and brought back to Manhattan. Shortly after my arrival, I was informed that I had a legal visit. Julia walked in, and I saw something that I hadn't seen yet.

Julia was crying.

We had a screen separating us. I wanted to hug her so bad but I couldn't. She continued to cry as she told me how worried she was. She said she went to visit me the previous morning and the prison staff said that I wasn't there anymore. They told her that the records showed that I was "in transit," but they didn't have any more information and they had no idea where I was. Julia said that she was afraid that I had gotten hurt, and that the rest of the lawyers on our team had been out searching hospitals looking for me. No one had any idea where I was.

She was frantic and she kept talking and crying, but then she said that she was so glad that I was okay.

"Gil, I'm convinced now. There are people who are trying to

make sure that we don't have a fair trial," she said.

We had an emergency court hearing before Judge Gardephe. Julia kept getting choked up as she tried to explain what happened and she put her hand on my shoulder whenever she referred to me. She told the judge that I was moved without anyone's knowledge. Never before, she said, has an inmate been mysteriously transferred to another facility without their lawyer's knowledge just days before the start of a trial. The judge asked the prosecutors if they knew what had happened, and Randall Jackson denied any involvement. Of course they were involved. They weren't ready to go to trial yet, so they inconspicuously had me moved so that we would lose time to prep. Unfortunately, it worked.

Judge Gardephe seemed upset and perplexed, and ordered me immediately back to the Manhattan facility where I had been for the past three months. Julia said that since we had lost two days, we had to delay the trial. Instead of going to trial in three days, I had to now wait another five weeks. The hearing ended and I was escorted back upstairs. As the nice female corrections officer who gave me the pen and paper weeks earlier walked me back to the cell, I sighed.

"Home sweet home," I said.

"Valle, this is not your home."

I lay down in bed frustrated. It had been around eighty days now that I was all alone. I still hadn't seen or spoken with my family, and I spent much of the rest of the day crying. All of my legal paperwork was gone, God knows where it was. I was back to having nothing and all of the momentum I had was taken away because of the shady business of the U.S. Attorney's office.

9.

Since the trial was delayed I told Julia to take a few days off. We were all incredibly stressed out and I could see it was taking its toll on her. I was relatively fine after the U.S. Attorney's office had me kidnapped, but I was still extremely upset about it.

Over time, I had developed a cordial relationship with the chief psychologist at the prison, who offered to stop by my cell at least once a week so that we could talk. I really appreciated her visits and found it helpful to talk to her. She made sure that my paperwork went through so that I could finally get a phone call and visits from my family. Up until that was finally taken care of we were only able to write letters to each other. The letters were tough to write because as much as I was struggling emotionally, I wanted to portray toughness at all times as I didn't want them to worry, so I was never really honest with them with regard to how I was feeling. At the same time, when I read their letters, I would wonder if they were really doing as all right as they said they were. I wondered how they were handling that their co-workers, friends, neighbors, the press, and everyone else in the outside world thought of their son as the "Cannibal Cop," while I was shielded from all of that.

The first phone call I made to my family was on a Sunday night in late January. I was allowed just fifteen minutes and it would be my only phone call for thirty days because I was housed on the same unit where other prisoners were assigned as punishment. It wasn't fair, but I was subject to the same rules as the rest of the prisoners in my unit.

Everyone met at my little brother's apartment and I was able to talk to everyone for about three minutes. Much like the letters, we all probably said that things were going better than they really were, but it was so nice to hear everyone's voices. The fifteen minutes went by way too quickly.

One week before the trial, in mid-February, they were finally able to visit me. We had a whole hour so that was much better. It was weird to see my mom and dad together. Naturally, my dad wanted to talk about my financial situation. I gave my little brother power of attorney privileges so he was handling my bank accounts and just doing an amazing job. Fidelity Investments, where I had contributed to my Roth IRA every year, had written a letter saying that because of my activities, they no longer wanted to keep my money and they closed my account before I even had my day in court. So much for innocent until proven guilty.

My family also told me that they had paid off all of my student loan debt (around $16,000) and my credit card debt (around $2,000).

"That way, when you get out, you can have a whole new beginning and just start over," my little brother said. It was so unbelievable and I choked up. What a family I had. Later that day, Julia stopped by and I told her about the visit with my family.

"They did something right when they raised you," she said. "The way you have been able to hold it all together, it's a testament to your strength and to the way they raised you."

Every few days the prosecutors were sending us more

paperwork. We now had a list of witnesses who they were going to call to testify. It looked like Kathleen was going to be the first one on the stand. Obviously, since she had found everything, she was going to be a very important witness for them. I didn't think she would be up there for long. I thought that she was going to testify about how she found everything and that would basically be it. I never treated her badly, I never hit her or the child, heck, I never even raised my voice to her. On top of that, according to the FBI interview notes that were turned over, she told them that she felt that life with me was going very well up until September 2012 when she found everything. Julia warned me that they were going to try and portray me a certain way, but I didn't take that too seriously, because there was nothing in my marriage to spin in a negative way. I know that we were both happy before all of this happened, and she confirmed that, at least when she sat down with the FBI. What could she say?

My initial thoughts were confirmed when we received transcripts of the grand jury hearing that led to my indictment. We were entitled to see the grand jury testimony of anyone who was going to be a witness at the trial. Kathleen basically walked them through how she installed the spyware, what she found, and that was it. I did notice something unrelated to Kathleen that was very interesting though.

In addition to the witness list, there was another list containing the names of everyone who was somehow connected to the case. This was for jury selection. Potential jurors had to let Judge Gardephe know if they had any connection to anyone on the list. It was very long; every woman who had been interviewed by the FBI was on it, as well as every member of the FBI who was a part of the investigation. There were well over a hundred people on the list. There was one name missing though. FBI Agent Rocky Warden. He was with Foto most of the day, and he was the one who left my loaded gun with me, unattended.

I thought it was weird that there were names listed of agents who I never saw, but yet his name was left off of the list. I casually mentioned it to Julia who also thought it was interesting.

It didn't take long for us to connect the dots. There was nothing turned over from the grand jury testimony from anyone about that supposed evidence that placed me on that woman's block. That myth had seemingly been debunked, and the U.S. Attorney's office knew it. Rocky Warden was left off the list of everyone who was connected to the case because he had to be the one who testified at the grand jury. No other reasonable inference is possible. If that is true, then he lied under oath about evidence that they never had. Since he wasn't going to be a witness at the trial, or connected to the trial in any way whatsoever, they didn't have to turn that testimony over to us. It was fishy.

If our suspicions were correct then an FBI agent committed perjury. During a pretrial hearing one of my other attorneys brought this up to Judge Gardephe. Since grand jury testimony is protected, the judge could not be compelled to force the U.S. Attorney's office to turn over the testimony from Agent Warden. In layman's terms, there has to be proof of some kind of bombshell to force a judge to open up that particular piece of the grand jury. The problem for me was that the bombshell was IN the grand jury testimony.

Then again, maybe it wasn't really a bombshell. These people had clearly demonstrated a propensity to lie in order to keep me detained at all costs, but I was convinced now that in the case of *United States of America v. Valle*, a crime had actually been committed. An FBI agent committed perjury and the U.S. Attorney's office was now covering it up.

Although that is speculation, I am likely correct. The sworn criminal complaint signed by Agent Foto, however, is not speculation:

"ANTHONY FOTO, being duly sworn, deposes and says that.... GILBERTO VALLE, the defendant, made and/or received cellular communications on the block in Manhattan on which [victim's] apartment building is located."

Everybody involved in the case at this point knew that Foto's sworn statement wasn't true. It does not matter whether or not it was an intentional lie or a mistake. A law enforcement officer cannot make a mistake like that in a sworn statement under oath. I recalled an NYPD officer who I worked with indicating in a similar sworn statement that he had recovered a knife from a defendant's right pocket. Surveillance footage of the arrest however showed that the knife was recovered from the left pocket. The prosecutor in that case was thinking about bringing perjury charges against the officer because of that seemingly simple mistake, but that to me demonstrated how serious police officers need to take their paperwork.

Here, in federal court though, that didn't matter. The U.S. Attorneys and FBI agents could write and say whatever the hell they wanted with carte blanche. I knew from day one that they were lying, now we had proof, but the feeling in the United States Courthouse was that this was just business as usual. Yes, they lied, but so what? I was just supposed to deal with it.

There were a few more pretrial hearings that involved what could and couldn't be talked about during the trial. Because of spousal privileges, the text messages between Kathleen and me during our marriage were not going to be used. This was a disagreement between Julia and I. She didn't want to use them because after Kathleen left, I lied to her and texted her that I never used photos of her. I thought my explanation as to why I did that made sense, but I went along with what Julia said and we decided not to use them. I thought that they wouldn't be needed, because Kathleen was supposedly only going to testify about what she found on the computer and how she found it. I never got what Kathleen and the prosecutors' position was on the text messages, but I have to think that they would have excluded them because they painted a good picture of what life was like in our home while we were together.

The judge also ruled that: "The government would not be permitted to elicit evidence of Mangan's mental state, because her mental state is not relevant to any issue in this case. Mangan will likewise not be permitted to offer an opinion concerning Valle's mental state, including whether he intended to kidnap her or other women."

There were other complicated exclusions involving cached images on my computer. The prosecutors wanted to show the jury very graphic pictures depicting blood and gore from the Dark Fetish Network but since it couldn't be proven that I had actually seen those photos, the judge ruled that they couldn't be shown. I hadn't seen those pictures anyway. Blood and gore isn't my thing, but since they were on the website they had been stored on my computer whether I actively looked at them or not.

One more ruling of note was that the prosecutors were not allowed to use the fact that I was a cop to their advantage. I was not to be held to a higher standard merely because I was a police officer.

Judge Gardephe said, "The defendant's status as a New York City Police Officer does not lessen or increase the government's burden of proof. Stated another way, the defendant is not held to a higher standard because he is a police officer. As with any other individual charged with a crime, the issue is whether the government has met its burden of demonstrating each element of offense beyond a reasonable doubt."

When alone in my cell, I started getting more and more nervous as we got closer to the trial. It wasn't because I thought I would be convicted and then spend the rest of my life in prison. Despite how dishonest the FBI and U.S. Attorney's office were, I still had faith in the system. I also had faith in myself. I knew I hadn't done anything that I was accused of.

My nerves were shot because I wasn't sure how I would be able to handle the embarrassment of the whole thing and I wasn't sure how I would be able to handle testifying. I was going to be honest, I had no choice, but talking to the whole world about my sexual interests was going to be a lot more difficult than talking to Dr. Dietz. I could not think of many more distressing things a person could be forced to do. It was going to be humiliating.

Of course suffering through all of that would be worth it, because I would be going home in a couple of weeks, and people would forget about it soon enough. The most important thing was that everyone would know I was innocent. It was going to be over, and I could start to pick up the pieces of my life and move on.

I thought a lot about my job. I hadn't been fired. The NYPD, as is their procedure, was waiting for the criminal case to play out. Once I won that, I would probably be subject to a Police Department trial but I did not do anything that warranted me getting fired. Although with the stigma now attached to my name, I wondered if I could seriously be a police officer again. Someone was going to call 911 and have the Cannibal Cop show up? But that was something I would figure out when I was home. All of the things with my job, my relationship with Kathleen, seeing my baby who I missed very much, all of that could be dealt with in a few weeks when I was home. There was nothing I could do in prison.

The first day of the trial finally arrived. My family brought over a few of my suits to the Federal Defender's office. That was good because wearing a prison jumper wouldn't look good in the eyes of the jury.

Two U.S. Marshals were assigned to pick me up from the prison and bring me to court every day. There was a back room somewhere in the courthouse where I was kept with my ankle chained to a twenty-five pound weight while I waited. Before the opening arguments there was supposed to be an evidentiary hearing without the jury present. The judge was going to decide, once and for all, whether or not the cell site evidence was admissible.

The prosecutors made that easy. Unfortunately the courtroom was relatively empty for the hearing, but after three months of stating verbally and in writing that they had evidence that put me on someone's block, then saying I was "in the vicinity," then saying I was within five hundred yards, finally, just minutes before opening arguments, Randall Jackson stood up and told Judge Gardephe that they would not be using that evidence during the trial. Of course they wouldn't, because they had no actual evidence. It was all a fictional story that rivaled some of my own.

It was one more big win for us before the trial started. One after the other, the claims made by the prosecutors after I was arrested were being proven to be completely untrue. People were starting to understand what really happened. Julia told me that there were some people in the media pulling for us. When the hearing was over the two marshals brought me back to that room and chained my ankle to the weight again.

About an hour later they walked me back to the courtroom. It was the biggest crowd we had seen yet. The back wall was filled with people standing and every seat was filled. My family was in the second row behind the defense table which was covered with binders and files. Julia sat to my right and to my left were three other lawyers and Alex. At the prosecutors' table were Agent Foto, a paralegal, Hadassa Waxman, and Randall Jackson.

There was some commotion behind us. I turned around and saw people shoving each other over a seat. This was an absolute spectacle that was beyond description. All of this because I used to mess around on the Dark Fetish Network? The bail hearings were crowded but this was something new. I made a conscious effort after that to just look straight ahead. I took a deep breath, and to my right, Julia was scribbling something down.

"You're going to be really great," I said. For once I wanted to give her a little encouragement. She laughed and said thanks.

I had a pen and a yellow legal pad in front of me. I was tapping the pen on the table and my mind drifted for a moment. I thought of the O.J. Simpson case. He had a yellow legal pad in front of him, and during the trial, somebody came out with a spoof, that joked about what O.J. was writing on the legal pad. I remembered this funny drawing of Judge Ito, and then I was snapped back to reality when Judge Gardephe entered the courtroom.

The jury entered shortly after that. These were the people that were going to figure out what happened and set me free. Julia was going to make them understand. I had no doubt about it, but I had to wait for a bit since the prosecutors got the first crack with the jury. Randall Jackson stood up, walked towards the jury box and blatantly disregarded one of Judge Gardephe's pretrial rulings with the very first words out of his mouth. He also set the pattern for the rampant prosecutorial misconduct that was going to occur over the next couple of weeks.

He told the jury in his booming voice: "There is a thin piece of metal that some members of our community are privileged to wear close to their heart. Some call it a shield. You may know it as a police badge, and it is the mark of an individual sworn to protect other members of the community. What you are going to learn during this trial is that Officer Valle chose to desecrate the trust that his community had placed in him."

So much for not holding me to a higher standard. He went on, absolutely railing on me. I tried to tune all of it out and just look forward to Julia's first chance to talk to the jury, but it was tough and I could not help hearing pieces of it. He told the jury that they would hear about my post-arrest statement to the FBI and that it was "chock full of lies."

I hated being called a liar and I especially hated it when it came from someone who was representing the U.S. Attorney's office, who had no problem lying from the very first bail hearing. Moreover, the *only* thing he was going to accuse me of lying about – as opposed to "chock full of lies" – was the situation involving whether or not I was on that woman's block and just a short time before his opening argument, he had abandoned the evidence they had claimed for months that they had.

When he was finished I was fuming. Then Julia got up there and set it all straight. She started off by telling the jury that what they had just heard, of course, was very disturbing and scary.

"But you know what is even scarier? Being charged with a crime that you didn't commit."

She went to explain the "journey" and lay out our case beautifully and logically. The jury would not be able to conclude that my behavior was anything more than fantasy role-play, she said, because it would be so painfully obvious to them. There were no steps taken by me in the real world to further a non-existent conspiracy and there was never any personal information provided by me or any of my "co-conspirators."

I felt a lot more relaxed when she was finished. Our side was telling the truth, and the truth was going to prevail. I thanked her when she got back to the table and told her that she was amazing. In twenty minutes, I had already experienced a roller coaster ride of emotions. Then Judge Gardephe asked if the government was ready to call its first witness. They were.

"The government calls Kathleen Mangan," Hadassa Waxman said.

And there she was. For the first time since the day she was

crying in our apartment after she had found everything, I saw the woman I fell in love with. She raised her right hand, swore to tell the truth, and sat down on the witness stand. She refrained from making eye contact with me.

You could hear a pin drop in the courtroom.

10.

It was tough to see her. All I could think of was how sorry I was that she was up there because of my behavior. She looked even more beautiful than I remembered. I felt terrible. She was wearing a pink shirt. In our three years together she hadn't worn pink once. As much as I hated to think it, it did make me wonder if that was a calculated decision by the prosecutors to have her appear more sympathetic to the jury.

Hadassa Waxman started the questioning. Kathleen described to the court how she found out about what I was doing, and as she did, I quickly realized that I should have taken more seriously Julia's warning about how they were going to portray me. Waxman asked her about our relationship, Kathleen started off by saying that in the beginning it was fun. She testified that I held doors for her, pulled out chairs for her, and acted like a total gentleman.

But then she began to describe a very different relationship from the one we had actually been in. Conveniently for the prosecutors, she testified that she noticed a suspicious change in my behavior beginning in January 2012. Of course that would be when it started, because the prosecutors were charging me with a conspiracy that began at the same time.

She testified about two very dubious episodes. The first one was the suitcase incident. Kathleen said I came home from work irate with her one night in February when I found out that she had thrown away an old suitcase of mine. This was supposed to fit with the government's case because in one of the fantasy role-play chats, I was going to kidnap a girl and transport her by stuffing her in a suitcase.

Of course, it *had* to be that suitcase. It was like Kathleen throwing out that suitcase foiled my evil plan to kidnap the girl. It wasn't like I could just go out, and you know, buy *another* suitcase if I was really going to do it. Kathleen and Hadassa Waxman had just tried to tell the jury that she prevented a kidnapping by throwing away that old suitcase.

What really happened was Kathleen, randomly and unannounced, went through my closet while I was at work to clean it up and yes, she did throw that suitcase out. I came home and I thought that was kind of odd, but I never yelled at her. My attitude was "Okay, whatever" but I did let her know that her doing that was a little weird. That was it, and we never spoke about it again.

The second incident she testified about was when she started to go jogging at night. She testified that I encouraged her to run at night, which was news to me. On my days off and after she put the baby to bed she would go for a run. She wanted to be around during the day to take care of the baby. Kathleen went on and testified that she found it incredibly weird that I asked her which way she was running when she was out. Can you believe that? I had the nerve to ask my wife out of curiosity the route she took when she went running. Clearly I am a sadomasochistic maniac. The message to the jury was apparently that I was going to communicate her jogging route to a co-conspirator. That scenario was never played out in any of my fantasy chats, but I gave Kathleen and the U.S. Attorney's office an A+ for creativity.

For the sake of clearing this up and finally getting it on the record, we lived in a neighborhood with some steep inclines up certain streets. I was just wondering if she was running up those inclines and pushing herself or just sticking to flat ground. Me asking her that was now "evidence" that I was furthering a supposed kidnapping conspiracy.

I was furious sitting there listening to this crap but it also showed how desperate they were to try to find anything, no matter how silly it sounded, because they had absolutely nothing other than fictional chats. They moved on to the PBA card that she gave to her old teacher friend. Kathleen testified that she thought that was odd too, but in reality it was all her idea and the friend was thrilled to get it.

Earlier I described the night her water broke. I was in the dog park with Dudley, totally freaking out and she was calming me down. After I brought the dog to my mom's, I was back in our apartment ready to go and she told me to relax and if I wanted to, I could take a quick shower before we left.

While on the witness stand, Waxman asked her very directly, "What did your husband do after you told him that your water broke?"

"He. Took. A. Shower." She said it in such a way as to make apparent what a totally "awesome" person I was. They left it at that, and moved on to the next thing. Kathleen continued to lambaste me. She portrayed me as a total deadbeat who didn't care about his family. No mention was made that Kathleen always told me that I was a great dad, no mention of how hard I was working so that she could be a stay at home mom. So Kathleen testified that in January she noticed my behavior starting to change, which lined up perfectly with the government's conspiracy charge. But in February we got engaged and in June we got married. After we got married, six months into the "conspiracy" and six months after Kathleen supposedly began to notice that I was a misogynistic dead beat, I got a new iPhone. Here are some of the text messages exchanged between us, a newly married husband and wife:

JUNE 25

Kathleen: "I'm having a hard time. I got spoiled spending all that fun time together now I'm all sad that you're gone. Damn job and all that responsibility.

Gil: "Sorry I got called in. I really enjoyed it too."

JUNE 28

Kathleen: "I love u x1000 just for going out tonight to make me smile :)"

JULY 2

Kathleen texts a selfie of her and our daughter while I am at work with the caption, "We love you!"

JULY 3

Gil: "Brooklyn Cyclones at 6 tomorrow?"

Kathleen: "Sounds great!!! What a fun 4th! Little family adventure! Uh it looks like it will be Midweek Mayhem and we will get to run the bases. We're doing it. It will be awesome."

Gil: "Nice! Cheap tix?"

Kathleen: "$16/person. Can't beat that."

Gil: "Good. I'll buy them when I get home."

JULY 8

Kathleen: "How are you feeling? I've been thinking about you all day."

Gil: "100 percent better but very busy again."

Kathleen: "Well thank goodness at least you're feeling well while u have to deal with their crap. Stay safe."

JULY 9

Kathleen: "How was court?"

Gil: "Haha trial got pushed back and I still get to come back tomorrow for another waste of time."

Kathleen: "And you get to be here in the afternoon to clean out ur closet. Wins all around! It fell open again. It was very traumatic. Women and children screamed and fainted."

Kathleen: "Oh come on! That was funnyyyyyyy."

Kathleen: "We have a tooth! And she's really crawling!!! Huge day!"

Gil: "Wow awesome can't wait to get home!"

JULY 24

Kathleen: "OF COURSE on laundry day she poops all over her crib again. Ugh! Whyyyyyyy!? *raises arms in agony*"

Gil: "Hahaha that sucks."

Kathleen: "Porqueeeeee?! Lol"

AUGUST 11

Gil: "What kind of vinegar? I'm at the supermarket"

Kathleen: "I just got a text from you about vinegar????"

Gil: "Yeah there was a shopping list in the kitchen. I got white distilled vinegar and some of that fag yogurt you like."

Kathleen: "Ur good to me. And it's FAGE!"

AUGUST 15

Kathleen: "We have clapping! It is EXACTLY as adorable as we'd have hoped :)"

Gil: "Wow awesome!"

Kathleen: "I will give you a million dollars if u come home with literally any type of ice cream and cookies."

Gil: "Otay"

Kathleen: "Ur da best:)"

You can decide for yourself whether or not this was a deteriorating relationship and whether or not Kathleen noticed suspicious behavior six months before these messages. For me sitting there, it was clear that Kathleen was committing perjury. The only people who truly know that though are Kathleen and me. Maybe those text messages are good enough for you to believe me.

The text messages sure would have been useful, but as I said earlier, we chose to not use them. I definitely wish we did, but I am not sure Kathleen and/or the prosecutors would have wanted them used. Hadassa Waxman then began trying to get Kathleen to say that she thought I was seriously going to murder her, which was in violation of Judge Gardephe's pretrial ruling. It was clear from what Kathleen was saying that given the opportunity, she would have said something like that. Julia must have gotten up and objected over ten times, and one time she asked the judge to please demand that Waxman obey his pretrial ruling.

Ultimately, Kathleen didn't say anything that would have pushed the jury to convict me. Her portrayal of our relationship didn't matter as far as the case went, but it mattered to me and it was deeply hurtful. I channeled the anger I was feeling towards the FBI and U.S. Attorney's office. They scared the daylights out of her and coaxed her into what to say, but still she was the one who chose to go on the stand and give that completely inaccurate portrayal of what life was like in our home. .

Julia cross-examined her and a more accurate picture about our relationship was painted. Kathleen described how we made decisions together as a family and she told the jury that I didn't abuse drugs or alcohol, and I was never violent or threatening to her or our baby. Julia then showed Kathleen pictures of her, our baby, and me while asking her to describe what was happening in those photos and she broke down crying hysterically. So did I. We were both crying so loud that the judge had to order a recess. I was an absolute wreck. I had my head down on the table and was crying in front of everyone. Julia put her hand on my shoulder and said that she had to show the pictures. I knew she had to, and they did what they were supposed to do. When Kathleen came back on the stand, she looked at me. I mouthed to her, "I am so sorry," and she broke down again. It became an absolute mess. It was the most difficult part of the trial for me to get through. I was angry with her, but I also felt so bad for her.

It was finally over after a couple of hours. The next witness was one of the other alleged "victims." That was a non-event. She didn't say anything bad about me and didn't make anything up, and day one of the trial was over.

The marshals walked me out of the courtroom and back towards the prison. One of them mentioned that it must have been really tough for me to see my wife up there like that. I was glad that they broke the ice, and over the next two weeks I would start to get comfortable talking to them. They seemed to be pulling for me.

I hadn't slept in days and I didn't sleep that night either. All I thought about was Kathleen. I thought about our first date again and all of the chemistry we had. I ended up going through the whole timeline of our wonderful relationship and I felt awful that it had come to this. I hated myself for letting this happen. I didn't do anything criminally wrong, but still it was my behavior that led to all of this. I kept thinking about what was going to happen when I got out. I was holding out hope that Kathleen would realize that she was lied to by law enforcement and I would tell her that I understood why she did what she did on the witness stand. I was hopeful that she would come around, and with time our wounds would be healed. She would get it, and she would turn her anger towards Hadassa Waxman, Agent Foto, and everyone else who played a role in scaring her. Somehow, some way, we would move on.

11.

I was functioning on no sleep as day two started. The first witness that day was Kate. Countless times over the years, I had fantasized about her being barbecued on a rotisserie. Now, here she was fully aware of that. Early on we made eye contact and then she looked down. She looked incredibly pissed off.

Despite her anger, she ended up being a very good witness for me. She said that she considered me a great friend, and that I never did anything that she deemed threatening. She said I was a non-violent person. Randall Jackson did the questioning, and out came the next huge reach.

Remember the PBA cards? I used to mail some down to my good friends in Maryland every year. Kate was one of them. Randall Jackson played on that and insinuated that I wanted to mail it to her so that I can learn her address as part of a plan to kidnap her. He showed her, the jury, and the rest of the courtroom text messages between her and me when I was talking about sending her the PBA card.

"Now, look here. He says, 'keep it hush hush.' What did you interpret that to mean?" he asked her.

"That he wanted me to keep it quiet," she said.

Of course, I said something similar to everyone I mailed a PBA card to. I had a lot of friends in Maryland, but a limited amount of cards so I didn't want anyone feeling hurt that they didn't get one. So I asked the people whom I sent the cards to please keep it under wraps. It was mind boggling that me giving friends PBA cards was being brought up as evidence that I wanted to kill them. Quite a stretch of logic.

Jackson then turned to my trip to Maryland when I met her for brunch. He brought up the text message I sent her when I said that I had driven past her work building, to which she responded "Yay!" He would argue to the jury that the message was proof that I was conducting surveillance on her.

When Julia went up for cross-examination, we got some great information out of Kate. In regard to our infamous brunch, Julia highlighted the full text message exchange we had. I texted Kate and told her that I was going to be down in Maryland.

"Let's plan some time to hang out!" she responded. I agreed.

"Lunch Sunday?" she asked. She then went on to pick the time and the place.

Kate testified that the brunch was pleasant. I was with my wife and the baby, and we talked about old college friends. She testified that I was good with the baby and that Kathleen and I seemed like we had a nice relationship. She also said that we got together whenever I was in town, which was four or five times a year. This was a far different story than what was portrayed early on. In denying me bail, the judges were told by Hadassa Waxman that Kate thought it was very weird for me to come down from New York to see her because we had been in very minimal contact over the years. Here was Kate on the witness stand telling the truth. She didn't lie about anything like my wife did.

I did mention the brunch to MoodyBlues, the guy I was talking to from England. That was the only time a real world event was mentioned in the fictional chats. But what happened after that? Nothing. We didn't discuss how that opportunity fell into my lap, and how I could use that weekend to abduct her. His response to me telling him that I was going to meet her for brunch was, "When you sit at her table you are going to fantasize that the meal isn't from her but form [sic] her! Lol!"

We ended up role-playing about her for roughly 20 more minutes, and then we went on to talk about other women. MoodyBlues started talking about a girl he was fantasizing about, and the upcoming brunch with Kate wasn't mentioned again until after it happened. I told MoodyBlues that she looked "mouthwatering," and the two of us didn't chat again for another month and Kate was never used in a role-play again. Again, as much as a fantasy like this may not be "normal" and might be shocking to many, it is no different than if I were to see a woman I knew for lunch and told a buddy of mine, "Man, she looked hot, I really wanted to bang her that day."

Next up was Melanie, the first girl I had fallen in love with in high school. Of all the women I ever knew, she was the woman I undoubtedly fantasized about the most. I had imagined her in every bondage position I could think of, gagged, and completely helpless at someone's mercy. Now it was her turn to sit on the witness stand and be a part of the show. This parade was devastatingly embarrassing for me, and God knows what it felt like for them. Other than Kathleen, who was understandably a wreck, the other women kept their composure just fine. I got the sense, or at least I hoped, that none of them actually thought that they were in any real danger. I kind of gathered that from their demeanor.

Melanie was an alleged "victim" because I had used the computer in my patrol car to run her name. I was charged with violating a federal computer hacking law for running her name. That was it, just one person. It wasn't 100 women whose information I recorded and stored like Hadassa Waxman and the FBI led everyone to believe after I was arrested.

I had run her name several times actually over the years. I ran a lot of people's names, my own, my brother's, my mom's, my dad's, Kathleen's, and others. I would run a name after I turned the computer on to test it to make sure it was working. In 2007, an NYPD officer was shot and killed at a traffic stop. The investigation into the shooting revealed that he had pulled the vehicle over and tried to run the license plate in the computer. The computer was on, but it wasn't working. Had the computer been working, the officer would have known that the car he had just pulled over was reported stolen. Instead, he approached the car without that knowledge and was killed instantly when he was shot in the head from point blank range. I vowed never to let that happen to me or my partner, so every single day after turning the computer on, I ran a name to make sure the computer was working.

Melanie was one of the names I had run on occasion. I had always cared about her over the years. What was somewhat funny was that on the criminal complaint, they had charged me for running her name in one instance in May, 2012. She had actually asked me to look something up for her. She had gotten into a car accident and she needed the report number. Instead of calling her precinct she called me, and I got it for her by running her name in the computer. She testified to that too. I wasn't supposed to do that, but cops use the computers like that all the time. It was nothing out of the ordinary.

The rest of her testimony was very much like Kate's. I was a friend to her and never did anything threatening. She described my romantic interest in her, but it was nothing bad. She said that the last time I had seen her, it was a pleasant get together.

Other than Kathleen, none of the other women who testified had anything bad to say about me. That's one thing that was so odd about this trial. The majority of the government's witnesses were actually helping me. The jury was aware of my online behavior, but what they were hearing from these women was that in real life, I was non-threatening and non-violent.

Once the women were done testifying, the prosecutors started to lay out their case. This was three straight days of sheer degradation for me. They called FBI Agent Corey Walsh who I remembered from the day of the arrest. He was the kid they used for the coffee run, and now apparently he was an expert on kidnapping. He was the one they picked to go up and testify about the investigation and how they had come to conclude that I was really planning to kidnap and eat women. Agent Walsh, at the time of my arrest, had been in law enforcement with the FBI for six months.

Agent Walsh testified that he and the other agents involved in the case divided my Internet chats into two groups: ones that they felt were fake, and ones that they thought were real. There were twenty-four total sets of chats. They deemed twenty-one to be fictional, and three to be real plans. His basis for separating the two sets was that if a group of chats had the word "fantasy," I wasn't actually committing a crime. If a set of chats did not have the word "fantasy," then it was a real bona fide conspiracy.

This method is imbued with a very basic logical error. It is known as the "fallacy of the inverse," and it is studied by anyone who is taking the LSAT. "*If A, then B*" does not mean "*If not A, then not B.*" Nevertheless, Waxman and Walsh went on and on, dragging it out by reading chat after chat into the record. For hours, my fantasy chats with anonymous strangers on the Internet were being shown on projectors as Walsh read them out loud.

"I will abduct her right out of her apartment, stuff her into a large piece of luggage after tying up her hands and feet and off we go."

"I am a little different though, I am a little more sadistic. I would want to see her suffer. I want to tie her up to a metal frame and slowly roast her alive until she dies."

"We're working on soundproofing the basement where she will be held captive and raped. We're planning on cooking her outdoors, no one is around for ¾ of a mile."

"I'm in the middle of constructing a pulley apparatus in my basement to string her up by her feet."

"The abduction will have to be flawless. They will be looking for her right away."

"I'm thinking of a Labor Day cookout with Kate as the main course at my place up in the mountains. I'll go to her place on Sept 2, kidnap her from there and we'll get her cooking Monday afternoon."

"My oven is around 5 feet long, 4 feet deep and 4 feet high."

"I really want her alive in the oven. I want her to experience being cooked alive."

To say it was humiliating is an understatement. I wanted to crawl into a hole. I did my best to tune it out. We had the trial transcript from the first day at the table, so I picked it up and just read Julia's opening statement over and over again. The day ended with Walsh on the stand, and the next morning he and Waxman continued.

One thing that I thought might be damaging were the chats I had with some guy from Pakistan or India. No one actually knew where he was from. At one point during a role-play, he asked me if I would really do what I was describing. I told him that if I were guaranteed to get away with it, I would. Under conspiracy law, my lawyers would later argue, that statement showed that I did not have specific intent to carry out the crime. The statement showed that I actually had not legally conspired because of the condition I identified, "If I were guaranteed to get away with it."

Legally, I was off the hook but I still wasn't thrilled about that exchange. It was said during a role-play, and as I explained earlier, constant disclaimers about the role-play being fantasy take the air out of the balloon. When this guy and I were communicating, it was understood that it was all fantasy but sounding as real as possible was what was titillating about it. Clearly there were never arrangements made for me to go to Pakistan or for him to come to the United States. No personal information was ever exchanged between us and there were weeks between chats. When we would chat again it was clear from reading the exchanges that we had forgotten about what had previously been discussed. It was like starting a brand new story.

Finally, we had our chance to cross-examine. Robert Baum took care of that for me, and it was a game changer. He started out with some obvious questions. He asked Agent

Walsh if any women had been kidnapped in this case.

"Thankfully, no" Walsh said. Julia chuckled next to me.

Then Baum asked if any women had been killed.

"Thankfully, no."

Had any women's body parts been found in my apartment, or in my oven?

"Thankfully, no" he replied again.

Baum then asked about Walsh's experience. He had no prior experience in law enforcement before joining the FBI, and he had no specialized training in psychology. Walsh said that he had never worked on a kidnapping case before and that he was not in a position to know how real kidnappers communicated with each other.

Then Baum got deep into the chats. He was able to highlight that the twenty-one sets of fantasy chats had virtually the same exact language as the three so-called real chats. Baum had Walsh read a line or two from one of the fantasy chats, and then have him read nearly an identical version of that line of two from the "real" chats. There were countless instances like this and many times these lines were about the same woman. But, according to them, one time it was fake and one time it was real.

It was also revealed that some of the alleged real chats did, in fact, have references to fantasy. Walsh read all of those into the record. Baum then went to the white van and the mountain house that I had talked about so much in all of the chats. He asked Walsh if any of these items, or any of the torture tools I described, actually existed. Walsh said no. Baum then asked him if I had an oven in my apartment big enough to fit a woman into.

"That would depend on the size of the woman," Walsh said. I laughed. Baum was absolutely shaming this rookie punk and I loved every second of it. At times, I heard people in the courtroom laughing. I took a deep breath and felt some sense of relief, it seemed like people were starting to get it.

During Waxman's questioning Walsh mentioned that there were kidnapping dates in the chats. This supposedly demonstrated that these weren't just fictional chats because we had discussed real dates to execute the kidnappings. Under cross-examination, however, Baum got out the fact that these dates would come and go and there would be no follow up. Neither the "co-conspirators," nor I would ask why the kidnapping never occurred. The next time we chatted we would start a new story.

Most amazing of all, under the FBI's working theory, I had "agreed" to kidnap three different women on one day. One was going to be lured to Pakistan, one was going to be kidnapped from Manhattan, and another one was going to be kidnapped from Ohio, all on February 20, 2012. Agent Walsh was able to assert that with a straight face, while there was more laughter coming from spectators. Even a couple of the jurors had smirks on their faces.

In a rousing, mocking voice, Baum asked one more time if any woman had been physically assaulted, kidnapped, or murdered, and began to imitate Walsh by yelling himself, "Thankfully, no!"

Hadassa Waxman shot up, objected, and asked Judge Gardephe to please instruct Baum not to answer a question for the witness. Gardephe had a smirk on his face and several of the jurors were laughing out loud. Gardephe gave the instruction to Baum, and they went on. It was revealed that the personal information I had sent about the women was not accurate, and that neither my "co-conspirators" nor I had ever communicated via phone, or ever even sought to attain each other's true identities.

The whole cross-examination, start to finish, was a home run. It could not have gone any better. At one point, there was a recess and Julia talked with some members of the press. Many of them had been completely convinced that I was being railroaded. Articles appeared the next day saying that it appeared that the case was a sham. We also found out that the FBI had MoodyBlues' backyard dug up because, you know, he told me that he had cannibalized people and buried the remains in his yard.

"Shockingly" enough, all of that digging yielded negative results.

Agent Foto testified for around ten minutes about the four hour post- arrest interview. The government cherry picked little statements here and there, like the line about my fantasy life bleeding into my real life. He didn't care to elaborate and explain that what I meant by that was that I was staying up later because I was chatting with MoodyBlues who lived in England. The fact that Foto, the lead agent on the case, testified for only 10 minutes was very unusual, Julia said. It was pretty much a non-event.

Their last witness was a computer forensic expert who essentially read my whole computer history including all of my Google searches. I had Googled all kinds of things because my stories were getting repetitive and I was looking for new ideas. Some highlights:

"How to cook a human"

"Best kind of rope to tie someone up"

"World's largest baking dish"

"How to chloroform a girl"

"How to prepare human meat"

"How to kidnap someone"

Really embarrassing stuff, sure. The government was arguing that these Google searches showed that I was serious about committing a kidnapping. But think about it. Would a trained NYPD police officer with a gun and handcuffs have to repeatedly Google "how to kidnap someone" to successfully carry out a kidnapping? And was I really planning to kidnap, kill, and then cook a woman in the world's largest baking dish? I searched things like this for new ideas for my chats and stories. I had numerous chat partners, but the same old stories were getting a little stale.

The government rested their case and another one of my lawyers, Ed Zas, argued to Judge Gardephe that the case should be dismissed. It was clear that the government had not come close to meeting their burden of proof. Instead of denying our motion, Judge Gardephe reserved decision. He would let the case play out, see what the jury did, and then decide what to do if they convicted me. He did make one important observation:

"There is almost no evidence of action by Valle beyond computer-based activities."

The "evidence of action" currently on the record? My brunch with Kate and the PBA card that Kathleen gave to her friend. I was feeling very optimistic. Julia approached me with a very important decision that we had to make. She told me they (the defense) were considering going on with the trial without me testifying. I was really surprised by that at first. We had done so much preparation, and it had been decided before the trial that the jury had to see me and hear me, so they would know I was not a monster.

But now, things changed a bit. Their case was so weak, and putting me up there would give them the opportunity to cross-examine me, and they would undoubtedly have me read all of the chats. There was no reason to put the jury through that again. Julia had consulted with other lawyers, and even a couple of people she trusted in the media. One of them said that she would be insane to have me testify.

During a recess, the marshals were bringing me back to my holding room. I was kind of cool with them now, and I asked for their input. Should I testify, or not?

"You know, from what I have seen in this case, I think less is more," one of them said.

Everything made sense. I told Julia that I wasn't going to testify. They were also 50/50 on having Dietz testify for a similar reason. The case was so weak and they wanted the jury to focus on the lack of evidence rather than be bogged down with science. So we decided that he wouldn't testify.

Our defense was over very quickly. There was a video deposition played of the guy who founded Dark Fetish Net. He talked about the cannibalism fantasy and how popular it is on the website and said that his website was not meant to be a criminal enterprise. I didn't think there was anything substantial one way or the other.

We had a retired cop take the stand and talk about PBA cards. He told the jury that cops give them out to friends and family all the time. Alex, the paralegal, also testified. She had created a Dark Fetish Net account and made a video showing how the site was navigated. She compared it to Facebook and said that DFN was just like any other social networking website, which technically it was. Randall Jackson cross-examined her and ended it by asking her if Dark Fetish Net had any mechanisms in place to prevent real crimes from happening. She said no. I asked Julia to go back up and ask Alex if Facebook had any mechanisms in place to prevent real crimes from happening. She went back to the podium, asked Alex that one question to which she responded "no" and came back to the table.

"Were you going to ask her that?" I asked Julia.

"No, that was all you. We're a team here," she said. That was my one contribution to witness questioning but it was a pretty good one. It made Randall Jackson kind of look like an idiot. When Alex left the witness stand, we rested our case. There was nothing groundbreaking, but we didn't need it. Robert Baum's cross-examination of Agent Walsh was the turning point.

The trial concluded with the closing arguments. In federal court, the prosecutor goes first, and then the defense, then the prosecutor gets to go again. Hadassa Waxman was up first and early on, she violated one of Judge Gardephe's pretrial rulings.

"Look at the way his wife, the person who knew him best, reacted when she read his words, when she saw his images, and when she learned of his plans for havoc and violence. What was her response? Did she say, oh, that's just my husband getting into some crazy stuff? No. She got out as fast as she could. She got out of there because this was not a sick joke. These were real plans for violence."

In other words, since Kathleen thought that my plans were for real, the jury should too. Since Kathleen was not allowed to testify about her mental state, Waxman did it herself.

Julia went up after Waxman and gave a passionate and genuine closing argument. She hit all of the main points that clearly showed nothing I did was part of a real conspiracy. It was all clearly fiction. She compared the case to that famous "War of the Worlds" radio broadcast when many people thought that America was under attack by aliens.

She implored the jury to read every single chat and they would reach the right conclusion. She acknowledged that the chats were graphic and that it should concern them that there are people who think these things, but in this country we do not convict people for having ugly thoughts. There were no real world actions, let alone a real conspiracy.

"This case has cost him everything. It cost him his wife. It cost him his adorable baby."

As Julia continued, I started to cry. I was thinking about Kathleen and my daughter again. I wanted this nightmare to be over already. I couldn't take being away from my daughter any longer. I couldn't take another night in a prison cell. I wiped my eyes with a tissue as Julia wrapped up, and when she approached the table I stood up and gave her a long, warm embrace. I thanked her for everything.

Randall Jackson got the last word. He began by berating Julia and he communicated to the jury that my sexual fantasy "is not a fantasy that is OK." He said that the pornography I looked at was "not normal pornography for any human being." Apparently he thought that people should be in prison for not being normal. He also played heavily on the police officer angle, which Judge Gardephe said he couldn't do:

"Officer Valle was a police officer in Manhattan and he walked around New York City with his police shield, his handcuffs and a gun. Defense counsel has been trying to sell you on two broad concepts that are in total conflict with your common sense. The first one is the idea that it is OK, a police officer, walking around New York City with a loaded weapon, who, on a daily basis, is engaging in making detailed plans about the execution of actual women. That is one of the underlying themes of what we just heard, that that is something that is OK. The second broad theme is this idea that you should somehow not be disturbed by the fact that this man, a police officer, walking around New York City every single day with a loaded weapon, has a primary sexual fantasy of seeing women mutilated and harmed in horrific ways, and that you should somehow not be bothered by that. There is nothing about Mr. Valle that is special. At bottom he is a dirty cop. It is something we've seen a million times."

He was arguing that they should convict me because to him my fantasies were not "okay." Imagine how full our prisons would be if fantasies were against the law. Jackson continued on, arguing to the jury that they should hold the fact that I didn't testify against me, "It is important for you to consider the fact that you heard no reasonable explanation of why he is risking his job, his freedom, his livelihood, his life. You heard nothing." Of course, according to the Bill of Rights, I did not have to testify and that could not be used against me. But in the world of the U.S. Attorney's office, anything goes. Convict at all costs, no matter what the truth is. Also, I never had any idea I was risking my freedom or my job. Why would I think that? To me I was just playing around on the net, and satisfying myself sexually, just like the vast majority of men do, or have done, at some point in their lives.

He went on to say that the mere fact that the FBI arrested me eliminated all reasonable doubt in my case, and he referred to me as a sexual sadist who was going to victimize a woman as soon as I had the opportunity, even though it was obvious to all that I had never done so prior. Then, out came this gem:

"Your common sense also tells you that you can't have a fantasy where you have unwilling participants in the fantasy. That doesn't make any sense."

So, next time you want to pleasure yourself while thinking of someone, make sure you ask for their permission first. If you don't, you'll end up in federal court in Randall Jackson's world.

He asked the jurors to put themselves in the shoes of the victims and compared my case to a hypothetical bank robbery and a hypothetical airplane hijacking where perpetrators had actually committed crimes. He invited the jury to think about being victims in those scenarios and said that they would be terrified. He did this in his trademark style, ranting and screaming in stentorian tones.

During all of this, Julia leaned over and was telling the rest of the defense team that this summation was very objectionable. They all agreed. They were dumbfounded at what was happening. At certain points, Ed Zas told her to object. Julia stood up and objected several times throughout the summation but Judge Gardephe overruled all of them. It was obvious to me that he wasn't allowed to say some of these things, particularly holding the fact that I didn't testify against me, but my defense team was on top of all of it.

Immediately after he finished, Ed argued for a mistrial based solely on Randall Jackson's grossly improper summation. Judge Gardephe denied it, so the case was definitely going to go to the jury. He read them the jury instructions, explaining to them the elements of a conspiracy and that the government had to prove all of the elements beyond a reasonable doubt. Listening to all of this, I was feeling good. There was no way a jury was going to unanimously convict me.

The jury was sent off for deliberations. I was mentally exhausted. I wanted to wait in the courtroom with my lawyers but the marshals wouldn't let me. I had to spend all of that time in that back holding room with my ankle cuffed to the weight. The first day went by, and there was no verdict. I was brought back to the prison, and walked back up to my cell.

After every day of the trial, when I was walked back to my cell, someone, whether it was an inmate or a guard, gave me encouragement. People inside the prison were able to follow what was going on with my case. When it finally got to the jury, I heard nothing but good things from other inmates. One guy across the hall told me he heard on the radio that I was going to win. Another one was wishing me well and telling me that I was going home soon.

It was amazing how much everything had changed from the day of the arrest. Most people understood now that I was being railroaded. I am generally not superstitious but it was hard then not to think about the coming days and about what I should say to the press. I was going to thank my lawyers and my family for their unwavering support, and I was going to call out the U.S. Attorney's office for their complete lack of integrity. Then I wanted to go home, tackle Dudley and spend the rest of the day playing with him. Then soon I could reunite with my daughter. I wondered if she was walking and talking yet.

I spent the second day in that holding room. Still, no verdict. Sometime after twelve p.m. on the third day, one of the marshals got a phone call.

"They have a verdict," he told me. My heart sunk. It was the most nervous I had been yet. He uncuffed my ankle and I was walked into the courtroom. This was it. I was finally going to go home.

I walked into the courtroom and sat with my lawyers. Julia was nervous.

"This is it. We tried a great case Gil," Julia said. I nodded and asked Robert Baum how he was feeling.

"I feel good!" he said.

"Bob, would you shut the fuck up? Just shut the fuck up!" Julia yelled. She was a nervous wreck. Ed Zas tried to calm everyone down.

"Whatever happens, either way, we are going to be fine," he said. That relaxed me a little bit, but only for a moment.

"All rise!" was yelled thirty seconds later and Judge Gardephe entered the courtroom. The jury entered shortly after that. Julia took a deep breath. No one in the jury made eye contact with me, and I didn't think that was a good sign. Then again, maybe they were just disgusted with me even though they acquitted me. Judge Gardephe asked the foreman if the jury had reached a verdict. The foreman said yes, then Gardephe asked him to stand up.

"What say you on count one, conspiracy to commit kidnapping? Guilty or not guilty?"

"Guilty."

In unison, Julia and I both dropped our heads. I was completely, utterly devastated. Later on, everyone who was there said that there was a loud gasp in the courtroom when the jury foreman said "guilty." I didn't hear it. I was in complete shock. This was a mistake.

They also found me guilty on the misdemeanor computer hacking charge. One by one, each juror confirmed that these were their verdicts. As they went down the first row, Julia took my hand from under the table and held it. She squeezed my hand as jurors numbers seven through twelve in the back row confirmed their guilty verdicts. It still hadn't hit me yet.

Judge Gardephe thanked them for their service in a case that "corrupts the soul." He dismissed them, and then scheduled a sentencing date. Before he left the bench he looked at Julia and me.

"I must say, I have never seen a defendant who received a more vigorous defense than that presented here, and I think that is obvious to everyone in the courtroom," he said.

Then he was gone, the marshals cuffed me and walked me out of the courtroom. Julia said she was sorry. I looked at my family. My dad had a look of disbelief on his face. My mom shook her head and mouthed to me that it was going to be okay. I held it together until the moment I left the courtroom, then, I completely lost it.

I couldn't move my legs, and I was crying hysterically. The marshals didn't say anything, but it was clear that they were in disbelief too. They let me have a moment to myself before they walked me back to the prison. The thought of me spending the rest of my life in prison entered my mind for the first time. I couldn't handle that. Maybe I would just commit suicide.

I was in a holding cell back in the prison while I waited to be taken back upstairs. I overheard a male prison guard,

"Yo, they convicted Valle."

"No fucking way! Get the fuck out!" a female officer responded. So they were in disbelief too. A couple of minutes later, someone opened up the cell door and there was the chief psychologist. I will never forget the look on her face that day. She was in shock.

"I just heard. Oh my God. From everything I saw, I thought you were going to win. I am so sorry," she said.

She walked me into a random office that was nearby and we sat down. I was frantic. I told her that I was never going to see my daughter again, and that I was going to spend the rest of my life in prison.

"This is my life now!" I kept saying.

She told me to slow down and take a deep breath. She told me that I was going from A to Z way too quickly, and that I wasn't at the part where I was going to spend life in prison. She explained to me the appeals process and she surmised that I had a shot. She asked me if I was thinking of hurting myself.

The thought that I had entertained a few minutes earlier left my mind in a millisecond. I was not going to take what I thought was a coward's way out. Even if I was going to spend the rest of my life in prison, I wasn't going to take my own life and put my family though that. I told her no, I wasn't thinking of hurting myself.

She spent about thirty minutes with me, and got me back to a decent place mentally. This part of the battle was over, and it was a setback, but I still had more fighting to do. There were measures in place to correct mistakes, and this jury's verdict was a really huge messed up mistake. Before she left she gave me a hug. I was walked back upstairs to my cell.

There wasn't much that was said by anyone. I was back in the cell just pacing around. The guy across the hall from me yelled out for me. I walked to the door and listened to him as he told me that he just heard some lawyer on the news say that he expected the verdict to be overturned on appeal.

"So, man up and keep fighting. Keep your head up and don't let them win," he said.

I was already feeling better. I knew this was going to be all over the news so I didn't want to listen to the radio, but I was so happy to hear what the inmate across from me said. I was doing all right for now. A few minutes later, two guards showed up to my door. They told me that they were ordered by the psychology department to place me on suicide watch.

I tried to tell them I was fine and that I wasn't going to hurt myself, but there was no shot. They said they were sorry but the psychology department has final say over something like this. They walked me down to the second floor and put me in the suicide watch cell. I had to take off all of my clothes. They gave me this Velcro suit that kind of resembled a bulletproof vest, but it was low enough to cover my balls. There was a bare mattress in the room with no sheets. An inmate at the other side of the window was assigned to watch me.

He filled me in a bit, and told me that he knew who I was. He said a lot of people on his unit knew about my case and that they all thought it was a stupid case. He also gave me some bad news. While I was on suicide watch, I was not allowed to make any phone calls or receive any visits. I was expecting Julia to come visit later that day, so that was a blow. But at least I had someone to talk to while I was down there.

When we finished talking, I laid down on the mattress. I had no control over the lights, and they had to stay on so that I could be observed. I thought about my family and wondered how they were holding up. I also worried about Julia. Then I thought about Hadassa Waxman, Agent Foto, and Randall Jackson. I despised all of them. .

These people were responsible for me, an innocent man, now facing life in prison. They were hell bent on having me locked up for life, and they lied their way through the whole case to ensure that would happen instead of accepting the fact that they screwed up and made a mistake. The right thing to do would have been to drop the case, but, in my experience, the U.S. Attorney's office in the Southern District of New York couldn't care less about justice or arriving at the truth. They only care about getting convictions, and it disgusted me.

I stared up at the ceiling and replayed it over and over.

"What say you on count one, conspiracy to commit kidnapping. Guilty or not guilty?"

"Guilty." Over and over and over, for the rest of the day.

12.

Thankfully they only kept me on suicide watch for one night. When the psychology department checked on me the next day, they concluded that I was not a threat to hurt myself. Shortly after being brought back upstairs, I was informed that my lawyers were there for a visit. I was so happy to see them.

My entire defense team was there. I gave all of them a hug, and, given the circumstances, we were all in relatively high spirits. They told me that they had tried to come the day before but they were denied access because I was on suicide watch. Julia said that she had gotten phone calls and e-mails from lawyers all over the country expressing their outrage over the guilty verdict. She even got a couple of phone calls from people in the U.S. Attorney's office telling her that the whole case was a travesty. I was surprised to hear that. Maybe there actually were honest people who worked in that cesspool.

There wasn't much else to talk about. They wanted to let me know that the fight wasn't over and that there was a lot that they could tackle with the post- trial paperwork. Since Judge Gardephe did not outright deny our request that the case be dismissed, he was still the one in charge. We were going to submit two legal briefs, a motion for judgment of acquittal, and a motion for a new trial. If the judge was going to rule in our favor in one of these, it would most likely be the motion for a new trial. The motions for acquittal are rarely, if ever, granted but we were going to give it a shot anyway.

They were going to work on all of that. They said my job was to just stay strong and try to keep my mind occupied. It was mid-March, and all of the paperwork wouldn't be in until the summer or so since the prosecutors would get their chance to respond as well.

My family didn't get to see me until the following Monday which was six days after the guilty verdicts. The defense team had reassured them that we had a good shot at getting a ruling in our favor mainly because of the lack of evidence, but also because of Randall Jackson's summation. Everyone was holding up better than I thought. Since baseball season was starting, I asked my brother to mail me a scorebook so that I could keep score of the Yankee games as I listened to them on the radio. That would knock off three to four hours a day. I also asked him to send me some LSAT prep books. My defense team, especially Julia, had inspired me to possibly pursue a career in law. I wanted to help other people the way she was helping me and I had to start thinking about life out of prison.

While I was able to occupy my mind some days, other days in prison were brutal as I waited for the paperwork to be finished. While, previously, I had some hope for reconciliation, not anymore. I wanted to divorce Kathleen, so my family retained a family court lawyer in New York. We served her papers the same exact week that she served me papers. Since she was in Nevada and I was a convicted felon facing life in prison, I had no ground to stand on. The terms they proposed were what was hers was hers, what was mine was mine. I was not allowed to contact her or our daughter in any way whatsoever. That last part was tough to take but my lawyer advised me that signing this document would not be a permanent thing and that once I was out of prison I could petition for visitation privileges due to a drastic change in circumstances. As difficult as it was, I signed off on it and Kathleen and I were divorced.

I got really angry whenever I thought about her testimony. I had copies of our text messages with me in my cell. I know that I kept secrets, and I should not have done that. I certainly didn't blame her for going to the police, but the way she portrayed life in our home really pissed me off. Still, I thought that she was lied to by law enforcement and the guilty verdict sure didn't help circumstances. She could now rest easy thinking that she did the right thing and did her part by taking a sadistic monster off of the streets. Instead of staying angry at her, I would funnel that anger towards the U.S. Attorney's office and the FBI.

I started to get random letters from strangers writing to me and offering well wishes and encouragement. They came from all over, including one guy from Iceland who wanted to know if French fries were my favorite food. It seemed that a lot of people were getting the fact that I was wrongfully convicted, and every bit of support helped. Julia gave me permission, and I wrote back to everyone.

In addition to "fan mail," I was also getting letters from people in the media. One of them was Daniel Engber, a journalist from *Slate Magazine* who had publicly been on my side from the beginning of the case. My defense team used to mail me his articles to show me that not everyone out there was against me. In his letter, he stated that he believed the verdict was wrong and he gave me his contact information if I ever wanted to talk. I asked one of the guards how I would go about sending e-mails from prison. He told me that I had to be in general population.

I had already been thinking about requesting a change to general population for a couple of weeks. It was roughly three months after I was convicted and it was getting very difficult not to have much human contact. My family came once a week but my defense team wasn't stopping by as frequently. I asked a lot of people what they thought about me going to general population. Everyone knows that cops are supposed to have a lot of problems with the other prisoners when they get in general population. The guards were kind of 50/50 about it, my family was nervous but they understood that I couldn't deal with much more of solitary confinement, and my lawyers thought it would be okay. So I requested a meeting with one of the captains.

A couple of days later, I was brought down to his office and we had a very nice chat. He began by saying he couldn't believe that I was convicted, and asked if I had good lawyers working on the appeal. He said he would be shocked if the guilty verdict wasn't overturned. Then I began to make my case for being moved to general population. He was concerned for my safety and gave me a counter offer. He could have me moved to a small unit at the Brooklyn facility, but I said that I didn't want that because my family was already accustomed to visiting me here and my lawyers were walking distance.

"I don't care if I get my ass kicked the first day," I said. "I have to give it a try."

He was reluctant but he agreed. He told me that if I have any problems whatsoever to tell one of the guards and they'd bring me back up to solitary. Later that day, I packed up all of my stuff and I was brought downstairs to a general housing unit. After roughly 205 days solitary confinement was finally over.

There was a big common area right in the middle of the unit, and as soon as I walked in, it seemed like everything stopped. Everyone was staring at me. People who were playing ping-pong stopped their game and watched. It seemed that even the ping-pong ball stopped in mid-air. It was clear that everyone knew who I was and I was pretty nervous immediately. My strategy was to just stay quiet and mind my own business.

The guard showed me to my cell and I met my cellmate. The unit that I was on was about half pre-trial inmates and half "cadre" inmates. Cadres had already been sentenced and they were finishing up their prison bids there. My first cellmate was one of those cadres and he was going home in a couple of months. Right up front he said that he knew me, and so did everyone else, but he didn't think I would have a problem there. I settled in, and then I went back out to the common area and watched TV for the first time in around eight months. The black inmates were in one corner watching something, the Spanish inmates were in another corner watching the Yankees, and everyone else was in the gym watching Spike TV.

I went with the Yankees, who were playing the Orioles that night in Baltimore. Although it was great to watch live baseball, I was on guard and constantly aware of my surroundings. Other than my cellmate, no one talked to me that first day, or the second day. I observed everything though, hoping that somehow I would be able to conform and fit in. Most people ended all of their sentences with, "You heard?"

The third day, I was sitting at one of the tables on my tier reading a book. Another inmate, who I hadn't met, sat at the same table and he was eating something. A few minutes later, out of nowhere, he said, "Keep fighting. You're going to win."

I thanked him, and then we got to talking about the case. He told me that everyone on the unit agreed that my case was the most bullshit case they had ever heard of. He also told me that even though I was an ex-cop, I didn't have to worry because I didn't work for the feds and I wasn't ratting on anyone. People who were ratting were the ones who had serious safety concerns there, he said. And yes, I was a police officer but I was also someone who was being railroaded.

Then after that, more and more people started to talk to me. It was funny how it worked out. It was like they all needed a couple of days to watch me and see if I was actually normal. I am sure my cellmate was saying decent things about me, and by the end of that week, I had a small circle of people who I was starting to befriend a bit. A common statement from people was something like, "We knew the case was bullshit but after meeting you, we knew you'd never do any of that stuff they were talking about."

People started to get comfortable busting my balls about the whole cannibal thing. They were never relentless, but I thought it was good that they felt comfortable enough to joke around with me rather than clam up and think that I was some kind of maniac. They treated me like one of the guys. There was a Muslim guy from England there who was always hilarious about joking around with me. He didn't want to eat his dinner one night, so he came up to me and passed me the tray asking if I wanted it.

"It's really good," he said. "It's pasta with some vegetables, and they put a few human fingers in there too."

The comic relief helped. As far as communicating with my family, things were much better. My e-mail account had been set up, and I now had 300 phone minutes a month.

Legal calls were free and I could call my lawyers whenever I wanted to without having to ask for permission. Though I never let my guard down, not for a second, I felt that I could survive in there while I waited for the post-trial aspect of the case to play out. I was trying to get good at chess, I was kicking people's asses in ping-pong, I went to Bible study every night, and I learned how to play spades.

I also started e-mailing Daniel Engber. He was becoming somewhat of an outlet for me to vent to. I trusted him fairly quickly. I told him that I was 100% innocent and I laid everything on him. I filled him in on everything that was lied about early on in the case and I elaborated on things like the cell site evidence that was never corrected in the media. I was very hard on myself at this point. I remember telling him that every morning I wake up wanting to throw my head through the wall for being so stupid. He kept everything we talked about confidential.

One day, he told me that he was in communication with a documentary filmmaker, Erin Lee Carr, who had taken an interest in my case and who believed that I was innocent. He passed along her contact information. I figured this could really help with the momentum of the appeal going in my favor. Erin and I introduced ourselves to each other. She said she was interested in making a documentary about the case for HBO and that she was shocked that someone could be sent to prison for what amounted to nothing more than a thought crime. Worse than just the thought crime, I said, was how much misconduct the U.S. Attorney's office engaged in throughout the case.

I was fully on board with Erin from the get go. I began to mail her some of the legal paperwork I had. I started off with the transcripts from the bail hearings. A week later, she got back to me and said that if someone blacked out my name and read the bail hearing transcripts, and then read the trial transcript, they would think that it was two completely different cases. She agreed that they lied. I began getting into how they used Kathleen to portray me to be something that I wasn't. I mailed Erin all of the text messages between Kathleen and me. Next time we spoke on the phone, Erin said that those text messages absolutely backed up my claim that we were in a happy relationship.

One day Erin told me about her father. He had been in and out of prison about eleven or twelve times, but he rebounded and had become a journalist for the New York Times. She said he wrote a book, so I asked my brother to send me "The Night of the Gun," by David Carr. When it arrived, I flew right through it. I had some hope that maybe I could parallel my life after his. Here was somebody who was a heavy drug addict and who had actually beaten women, but he turned his life completely around and was now a very well-respected and loved writer. If he could pick up the pieces of his life and rebuild after all of the crimes he committed, I certainly could rebuild mine when I hadn't even committed a crime. Maybe I would never be loved by the masses but this is a country of second chances. He got his and ran with it, and I was going to get mine.

That further cemented my desire to work with Erin. This man was her father, so surely she would appreciate the opportunity for someone to start over and have a new life. She also often said that she fully believed in my exoneration.

While I was full speed ahead with the documentary idea, the federal defenders weren't. What complicated things even more was that a professor from Fordham Law School, along with several of his students were now helping out with the post- trial paperwork. Professor Cohen seemed to be really aggressive about my case, and I was really in tune with him.

He was okay with the documentary. He agreed that we needed to get the truth about this case out there, and maybe it would put pressure on the judge to do the right thing. Julia and the rest of my defense team were against it. They didn't want to ruffle any feathers and they just wanted things to play out. There was a split in my family around this. They all had spoken with Erin already and most agreed that she sounded like she would do right by us. My mom was on board with the documentary, but my dad wasn't.

I began talking often to Professor Cohen on the phone, and he stopped by with his students for a visit. We seemed to be on similar wavelengths and I began considering firing the federal defenders. After all, they had lost the trial and I didn't sense as much aggressiveness from them as I did with Cohen.

I couldn't do it though. Julia had put her heart and soul into this case, and I knew that. At some point the professor wasn't around as much anymore. I had suspected that there was some kind of falling out between him and Julia. As far as Erin and the documentary, I still communicated with her at will, but I had not fully committed to the project.

In September, six months after the conviction, the paperwork for the post- trial motions was in. It was now up to Judge Gardephe. There was no definite timetable, but my defense team thought that we would definitely have a ruling by the end of the year. We never seriously entertained the thought of being granted the acquittal just because it almost never happens, but we were very optimistic about getting a new trial.

While we waited, another major group showed an interest in the case. The CBS show *48 Hours* had contacted my attorneys and they wanted to do a story about my case questioning the conviction. They visited me in prison with my lawyers and laid out what they wanted to do. They seemed to understand everything just like Erin, but Erin had an hour and a half to talk about the case and *48 Hours* only had forty something minutes, factoring in commercials, so I was still leaning towards her.

She started to come and visit me in prison with my family. The first time she was there, she came with my father. When I got to the visiting room, she was in the bathroom and my father started raving about her. He said she completely gets everything. Then I finally met Erin for the first time. She came right up and hugged me, which I welcomed, but I also thought was a little surprising. I hadn't met many women since I was arrested, but here was one who knew about and had read all of the fictional chats detailing acts of violence on women and yet, she came right up and hugged me.

We didn't talk too much about the documentary. She gave me the opportunity to tell her more about the case, and my father would jump in every now and then. The visit went very well, and when I got back to the housing unit I told the Muslim guy from England about the girl who wanted to do a documentary about my case.

"Next time, if you want, you can take a bite out of my arm before you go in. I wouldn't want you to get hungry around her," he said.

The ball busting was about to get even better. I wanted something else to take up some time while I was waiting for Judge Gardephe to rule, so I asked one of the counselors about getting a job. The only one available was in the kitchen. I was fully aware of what would happen if I took that job, but screw it, I signed up to work in the kitchen.

I worked on Sundays through Thursdays from 6 in the morning to around noon. The whole time, the guards who worked in the kitchen were really cool. For the first couple of weeks I worked on the line putting whatever food I had in front of me in a tray, then passing it along to the next guy. It was mindless work but it passed the time. I guess I did pretty well with that because I earned a promotion. I moved on from the line to the "carts." I made sure all of the food carts for all of the units had the right amount of trays in them.

Contrary to what people think because of some of the press my job received, I was never a prison cook. I cooked my own stuff every once in awhile and I started trying to make pizzas with soft tortilla shells as the crust. I cooked those for me and my co-workers and sometimes a couple of the guards would get a couple of slices.

One day while I was in the kitchen, that really nice female guard from the solitary confinement unit walked in. She apparently was unaware that I had a job in the kitchen.

"Valle, they put YOU in the kitchen?"

"Yeah, it's fine. The only rule is that once the ovens are turned on I am not allowed anywhere near them," I joked.

She let out a loud laugh and then asked how I was doing. She told me to never lose my sense of humor, and that she hoped everything worked out, and to sue the hell out of the government.

Meanwhile, the holidays came and went. As you can imagine,

Christmas was difficult again. My hope about this Christmas being different hadn't come to fruition. I thought a lot about my daughter. I wanted to send her something but the divorce terms prohibited that. Those were some really tough days and I didn't want to let my family know that I was having a hard time. I requested psychology a couple of times during the holiday season but there wasn't much they could do. I wanted to work a second job though so psychology hooked me up with a job as an Inmate Companion.

Part of the role of this job was watching people who were on suicide watch. I was on the other side of the window now, there if they wanted to talk. I also had to document what they were doing every fifteen minutes. Most people were just quiet and tried to sleep, but some did want to talk. It felt good for me to be there to help people again despite what I was going through myself.

My lawyers' prediction about having a ruling by the end of the year was wrong, but they thought it had to be coming soon. My relationships with some of the inmates were getting stronger and I was considering a few of them legitimate friends. The Muslim guy ended up going home and I was sad after that. He was a relentless ball buster but he always made me laugh and I missed him right away.

I was close with another guy. Before they locked it down at the end of the night I would usually go to his cell and talk. We'd talk about virtually anything, but he knew when I was feeling down and he was always there to offer encouragement. In fact, I let him read my post-trial paperwork.

"I keep telling you, you're going to win," he would often say. He wasn't just saying that I'd get a new trial; he was saying that I was going to be acquitted.

January passed, and then it was February. I had a new cellmate now and he suggested that I send Erin a card for Valentine's Day. There was a guy on the unit who made cards that could be mailed so I asked if he could put something together for me. He did, and I mailed Erin a card for Valentine's Day. Although I still hadn't committed to the documentary, I wanted to thank her for being on my side.

March went by, and then I had my 30th birthday in April. Some of the guys put a cake together for me. It was amazing what some of the people in there could do with the most basic ingredients. I wasn't much in the mood to celebrate, but the gesture was special.

There was still no ruling from the judge, and we had no idea when he would rule. It was tough not having a firm date to look forward to. I was feeling a bit abandoned by Julia and the rest of the legal team. They weren't visiting me anymore. I knew that there was nothing to update me on, but it still just helped to see them. My mom ripped into Julia on the phone one day. Soon after, Julia sent me an email.

"Your mom left me one message screaming at me, then left another one apologizing," she said. Then she went on to write a beautiful message about how they haven't abandoned me and that I was all she thinks about. I forgot who made the point, but someone told me that it has to be tough for her to visit me and see me in prison when she knows that I don't belong there. Seeing me is a reminder that we lost, and an innocent man was facing life in prison.

One day around this time, my father was supposed to be coming to visit me with Erin but when I got to the visiting room, Erin wasn't there. He told me that they wouldn't let her upstairs to see me and they weren't told why. After the visit, I called Erin. She sounded really pissed, and she said that they didn't give her any explanation whatsoever why she was denied a visit with me. All they told her was that she was no longer on my list of visitors.

I was outraged. This had to be the U.S. Attorney's office again. All phone calls and emails are monitored, so they knew that Erin was interested in doing a documentary that was going to clear my name. Just like when I was moved to Brooklyn unannounced before the trial, they were screwing with me again. I went to one of the guards who I really trusted and told him what happened.

"That's impossible," he said. They can't deny a visit without giving a reason.

I told him they didn't give her one. He said he was going to try to find out what happened. The next day he came up to me and he told me that something unusual was definitely going on.

"They told me that it's above my pay grade and to drop it. They wouldn't tell me anything else," he said.

So there was another blow. Erin and I could still communicate through e-mails but I liked seeing her. I felt comfortable enough around her now to joke with her and we seemed to get along great. Whenever this case ended and things went my way, I wanted to hang out with her on the outside. I considered her a friend, and it hurt me that she was removed from my visitor list without any explanation.

There was still no ruling in May, and still no word on when it was coming. It had been 14 months since the conviction now. One day, I was in the kitchen mopping up a spill and I thought to myself that this could be the rest of my life. It was extremely depressing. Later that night, my cellmate told me that he stayed out of the room most of the day because he knew I was in there crying. He knew me well enough now that he couldn't say or do anything to help. I just had to ride it out. As bad as things had been, they were getting even more difficult for me emotionally.

I requested psychology on June 19th. That was my wedding anniversary with Kathleen, and her birthday was coming up as well. Fathers' Day was around that time too. I was watching the Yankee game and they kept showing fathers with their kids in the stands. When I talked to my father later that night on the phone, he asked if I saw the game and he said that he knew I must have been crushed seeing all of those shots of the crowd.

I couldn't take much more of this waiting. When was it going to end? Julia and the rest of the team were also reaching a point of wondering whether or not it would be appropriate to ask for an update from the judge. The amount of time this was taking was incredibly unusual.

Law and Order SVU did an episode that was based on my case. The guy in the episode had actually built a torture chamber and met with Ice-T who was acting as a co-conspirator. They arrested him and it went to trial. The defense lawyer made a passionate closing argument talking about how we don't want to live in a world where our thoughts are prosecuted. The jury acquitted the guy, and I heard all about it for the next couple of days. Julia said that she hoped Judge Gardephe watches SVU.

Another month was about to go by. The morning of June 30th began like every other morning that I worked for the last seven or eight months. At 5:45 am, the guard on duty opened up my cell door.

"Valle, get ready for Food Service."

That was their fancy way of saying "kitchen." I brushed my teeth and put on my white uniform. I waited for the kitchen staff to pick me and my coworkers up and off we went to work, down the elevator to the basement. I put on a hairnet and started to prepare for the workday. Ramadan was coming up so there were some procedures in place that one of the guards was explaining to me. Then he stopped himself, and said, "I don't even know why I'm telling you this. You're going home soon anyway."

"Yeah, sure" I said. I had heard that enough already and I was getting tired of it. I was mentally and physically exhausted. This purgatory I was in was getting unbearable and even if the ruling didn't go our way, at least then we could move on to the Court of Appeals. I needed something.

At the end of the workday, around 12:30 p.m., I got back up to the unit and like I always did, I checked my e-mail. There was something from Julia. I clicked on the message and my heart sunk. She said that the ruling was coming that day.

I immediately got on the phone with her and she sounded exuberant. She put me on speakerphone so that I could talk to everyone. They informed me that there was a hearing scheduled for the next morning and that Judge Gardephe requested that Pre-Trial Services attend the hearing.

"That means it's a bail hearing, right?" I asked

They told me that they couldn't think of what else it could be, and it was promising. I was thinking that we won a new trial and that tomorrow morning would be a bail hearing.

Maybe I would be going home while I wait for the new trial. For me it was great news, but my heart was pounding the rest of the day. I called my family and let them know. I only had about ten minutes left for the month so I had to use them sparingly. I was frantic, checking my e-mail and calling. Surely, by the end of the business day, we would know. But at six p.m. there was still no word.

Julia said they were going to be staying in the office until they got a ruling and that I should check back every 30 minutes. Around eight p.m., there was still nothing, but Julia was told that the ruling was coming. Judge Gardephe's clerk didn't have any more information than that. I was praying that I would know by 9:30 p.m., because then I wouldn't have access to the phone or e-mail since that's when they locked us down for the night.

It didn't happen. I was beyond disappointed when I was forced to hang up on Julia at 9:30, and like she always did, she told me to hang in there and that she'll see me in court in the morning. Soon I was back in my cell for the night, wondering if possibly this was finally it, Twenty-one months had come and gone. I lay on my back in bed and just stared at the ceiling. Surely, Judge Gardephe wouldn't deny me bail again. He sat there through the whole case, and had said that very important line about there not being "evidence of action beyond computer based activities."

While I was locked in the cell, not getting a wink of sleep, the ruling had come down. My lawyers and my family had already heard the news. I didn't know this, of course, so I suffered through that night waiting for six in the morning when the guard would unlock the door. As it got closer and closer to six, my heart was beating faster and faster. Finally, I heard the sound of the key unlocking my door. It was the start of my 617th day in prison. I ran out of the cell and sprinted towards the computers. I typed in my login information and I had nine e-mails waiting. Julia's jumped out, because it was in all caps with about twenty-five exclamation points.

"WE WON!!!!!!!!!!!!!!!!!!!!!!!!!!!!!!!!!!!!"

13.

While I was locked in my cell the night before, Judge Gardephe issued his ruling. He wrote:

"None of the conspirators ever met or took steps to meet, nor did they ever speak by telephone. There is no evidence that the alleged conspirators ever exchanged telephone contact information or accurate information about the area in which they lived, or that they ever knew or sought to learn each other's true identities. Communication between the alleged conspirators was episodic and generally infrequent; months often passed between chats, with the alleged conspirators forgetting what had previously been discussed."

"The nearly year-long kidnapping conspiracy alleged by the Government is one in which no one was ever kidnapped, no attempted kidnapping ever took place, and no real-world, non-Internet based steps were taken to kidnap anyone. Moreover, neither Valle nor any of his alleged co-conspirators ever even raised the issue of whether a 'planned' kidnapping had taken place, and, if not, why not. Dates for 'planned' kidnappings passed without comment, without discussion, without explanation, and with no follow-up. The only plausible explanation for the lack of comment or inquiry about allegedly agreed-upon and scheduled kidnappings is that Valle and the others engaged in these chats understood that no kidnapping would actually take place."

"The details Valle provided to his alleged co-conspirators concerning the targets of the kidnapping conspiracy were –

as to identification information – all false. Valle lied about where the purported kidnapping targets lived, their last names, their occupations, their dates and places of birth, where they had attended or were attending college. Valle never provided his alleged co-conspirators with the last names or addresses that would have permitted them to locate and identify these women."

"Likewise indicative of Valle's lack of criminal intent is the fact that he provided his alleged co-conspirators with a veritable avalanche of false, fictitious, and fantastical information concerning himself and the steps he had allegedly taken to facilitate a kidnapping, including representations about a non-existent van that would be used to transport victims to a non-existent cabin, where they would be held in a non-existent soundproofed basement with a non-existent pulley mechanism, and cooked in a non-existent human size oven."

"The Government does not attempt to explain the 'vanishing plots' phenomenon repeatedly seen in the evidence at trial. If there was a genuine agreement to kidnap someone, and a specific intent to do so, it is inconceivable that the dates for planned kidnappings would repeatedly pass without inquiry, comment, or explanation from Valle or any of his alleged co-conspirators. Likewise entirely inconsistent with a genuine kidnapping conspiracy is Valle's expressed intention to kidnap three different women in three different places on or about the same day: February 20, 2012. The notion that Valle had resolved to lure [alleged victim #1] to India or Pakistan, while at the same time kidnapping [alleged victim #2] in Columbus, Ohio and kidnapping [alleged victim #3] from the Upper East Side of Manhattan, is simply outlandish."

"The jury's verdict on Count One, conspiracy to commit

kidnapping, cannot stand, and Count One will be dismissed."

Judge Gardephe went on and on and even commented on some of the prosecutorial misconduct during their closing arguments. Some people were saying that it was a miracle that I was acquitted, simply because a judge rarely takes that step, but if it was ever going to happen this was the case.

The rest of the e-mails that morning were from my family and Erin. Everyone was able to celebrate the previous night while I spent the night awake and pondering the outcome. When I read the e-mails, I was ecstatic, but I did not want to make a scene while I was still in the housing unit. I woke up a handful of the guys that I considered friends and told them that I was going home. I had been acquitted. Everyone shot out of bed as word was getting around quickly. Some people had the morning news on, and the story was breaking. The Cannibal Cop had been cleared and was being released from prison.

One of the guards told me to get ready for court while people continued to congratulate me and wish me well. It was surreal. It had only been about fifteen minutes since I got the news. I gathered all of the letters I had saved over the last twenty-one months and carried them down with me as I was brought down to the holding area one last time. The prison staff held on to the letters while I went to court.

When I walked into court my family was already there clapping. Several members of the press who had followed the case were also smiling and giving me their thumbs up. Erin was there with my family too. I walked to the defense table and hugged all of my lawyers. To my right, the people at the other table were clearly not happy. Agent Foto had a dumbfounded look on his face. I remembered that smug look on Hadassa Waxman's face when I was denied my final chance at bail, and the look on Foto's face now was just a beautiful juxtaposition.

The hearing was brief, but Hadassa Waxman vowed to appeal Judge Gardephe's ruling, so I wasn't completely out of the woods yet. The Court of Appeals could reinstate the guilty verdict and I would be facing life in prison if that happened. Judge Gardephe ordered me released but on house arrest pending the appeal. I thought that was wrong, but at the time I didn't care. I was going home. He also ordered that I go to therapy every week and I was not allowed to use the Internet. Although he acquitted me on the major count, he left the misdemeanor conviction for improperly using my patrol car computer in place so I had to be sentenced for that. Since I had already spent over a year in prison, the sentence would just be time served.

Right after the hearing, I was brought to Pre-Trial Services. They attached a monitor to my ankle and explained to me that I had to call in every Friday to check in. I wasn't allowed to leave my home except for legal visits and for therapy. They would also show up for random, unannounced home visits. None of this really hit me yet. I just wanted to go home.

I was released right from the courthouse so I didn't have a chance to get my letters. Along with my family and my defense team, I walked out of court a free man. The amount of media outside was insane. I walked up to the podium that was equipped with a whole bunch of microphones from the different media outlets and made a quick statement thanking my defense team for their hard work and apologizing to everyone who was hurt and offended by this case. This was almost too much to handle. My last moment of being a free man was twenty-one months ago, right before I was arrested in my apartment hallway. Now here I was standing at a podium with scores of cameras pointed in my face.

We all walked towards the Federal Defenders office while I was absolutely swarmed and surrounded by the media. They all began asking me more questions about the case, and what was I going to do with my life, but I didn't want to say anything else. I just kept saying that I was tired and I wanted to go home. We finally got to the office, and Erin and the people from *48 Hours* were there. We still had an appeal to worry about, but for now we were celebrating. We all drank a little bit of champagne, then they hooked my family and me up with a car service to get home. We left through a back exit to avoid the media swarm.

I couldn't believe it. The warmth of the hot July 1st day was so exhilarating. I was in the back of a taxi with my family. My mom wouldn't let go of me. I just stared out the window and enjoyed views that I hadn't seen in twenty-one months.

When we turned onto the block of my mom's house, there was a crowd of people already assembled in front. It was more media. My family got out first, then my mom opened up the front door. I exited the car to the sounds of photographers snapping picture after picture, then made it home. What happened next is something that I will never forget.

Dudley was confined behind double doors, and started crying like crazy when he heard my voice. My mom let him out and I dropped to my knees. He charged me and practically knocked me over. Obviously he didn't forget me. He was licking my face like crazy while I hugged him. I didn't want to let go.

It didn't take long for the doorbell to ring. That would

become a frequent occurrence over the next week. All day long, the press kept ringing our bell wanting to talk to me. My lawyers didn't want me talking to the press yet since the case was still pending, but sometimes my mom would talk to them anyway. They asked her what I was eating for lunch and dinner and she would happily tell them. After a few times, I asked her to please don't tell the *New York Post* and the *New York Daily News* what I am eating. They were taking it and running with it.

A couple of days after I was released from prison, I went to therapy for the first time. I was pretty nervous about traveling there, so my mom came with me. I kept looking around wondering if people noticed me. It kind of reminded me of those first couple of days in general population in prison. I found myself on guard. I sensed that a few people recognized me that day but no one approached us.

I appreciated going to therapy because it was really the only time I was allowed to get out of the house. My therapist explained that he was there to help me readjust back into society, not to discuss my sexual fantasies unless I wanted to discuss them. I got comfortable talking to him quickly. He was obviously familiar with my case and he communicated to me that the right outcome had been reached.

Finally, now that I was out of prison, I started to hear from some of my former NYPD colleagues. One of my best friends on the job was retired now. He told me that everyone supported me from day one but I never actually received any of that support. I understood it in a sense because the NYPD has a strict policy that cops are not allowed to associate with felons. That wasn't good enough for me though. If it were me on the outside, I would have found a way to support a person who I thought was being railroaded. Even if they couldn't support me though, my family was left completely in the dark. Not one person from the NYPD reached out to see how my family was doing, and when my lawyers went to the precinct asking for help, the cops turned their backs on them more than once. Cops who had committed acts of domestic violence would get representation and assistance, but they didn't have the time to talk to my lawyers while they supposedly supported me. That is something that always pissed me off, but I didn't shut the door on them.

Erin and HBO were still interested in doing the documentary, and so was *48 Hours*. I was under a lot of pressure from both groups to make a decision. Even though I had been acquitted and released, I sensed that there was still a lot of misinformation out there and people thought that I got off on some technicality. Erin told me that part of her job now was to help me clear my name. I chose Erin because I talked to her a lot more over the previous several months, I trusted her, and she had basically double the amount of time to highlight everything in the case.

I met with Julia and the rest of the federal defenders about doing the documentary. They were dead set against it and it felt like I was up against a firing squad. But I liked Erin. She was firmly on our side and she would do right by us. Julia acknowledged that there seemed to be something different about Erin and that she trusted her, but doing the documentary while the case was still pending was not a smart move. I relayed this meeting to Erin, and she asked if it would help if she sent over all of the questions she was going to ask as part of my interview with her.

Julia worked directly with Erin for a few days and they bounced the interview questions back and forth. Julia eliminated what she felt Erin could not ask right now, and

Erin was okay with it. I had another meeting with the lawyers and we reviewed the questions and my answers. They were still against me doing it, but I had put my foot down and they started to work with me on it.

Erin and her HBO crew visited me with all of their recording equipment over 10 times while I was on home confinement. There wasn't much going on for them to film. They wanted footage of me playing with Dudley and just doing normal things around the house. They filmed me watching TV and doing all kinds of banal things. Since there wasn't much to do, I often cooked for them when they were there. I thought it was a nice thing to do for them while they spent hours at my house. I was fully aware of how silly people could get with me cooking, but I figured Erin was above all of that.

During one of the visits I officially signed my contract with HBO. I wasn't allowed to talk to any other media outlets until the documentary aired and I agreed that I wouldn't be paid for participating. I didn't care. The money wasn't important. Erin and HBO were going to help me clear my name, and that was more important to me than any money I could realistically get.

Julia, Ed Zas, and Robert Baum all came over for the official sit down interview with Erin. Erin went through the questions that she previously provided to Julia and it was a breeze. Since she provided the questions ahead of time, I wasn't as stressed out as I might have been. After the interview, Julia gave Erin a lot of paperwork, including the letter that Hadassa Waxman wrote to Judge Gardephe before my last bail hearing, in which she explicitly lied about numerous aspects of the case. Erin appreciated that, and she said that the amount of lying they did was very important to what happened in this case.

During "non business hours", Erin and I would text fairly frequently, sometimes even well after midnight. I appreciated how hard she was working for me, and my mind even wandered towards some possible romantic involvement with her when everything was over. It couldn't kill a guy to try, right? Here was a woman who was totally fine with everything, texting me late at night, calling me "babe." Of course, my mind went there.

I thought often about Kathleen and my daughter. I had spoken with a couple of lawyers in Nevada and I was advised to wait until the appeal process played out. It didn't make sense to petition for visitation now because the case wasn't over yet. A judge out there could rule against me because of the possibility of me ending up back in prison after they grant me visitation and obviously that would not be healthy for my three-year-old daughter.

I often wondered what Kathleen was thinking. Was she realizing that she was lied to yet? Even though we were divorced, I still found myself wondering if there was a chance things could somehow work out. I had no idea and I was not permitted to talk to her yet. I was softening up on the fact that she testified against me. I was able to empathize and understand why she did it, but I was hoping now she was realizing that there was a whole other side to this story that she initially refused to listen to.

I was on home confinement from July to November. Pre-Trial services visited me a handful of times early in the morning but there was nothing to be concerned about. They were not a headache at all for me. It was getting old being on home confinement though. This whole idea of me being free, but not really free, was frustrating and I was getting cabin fever. In November, Judge Gardephe sentenced me to time served for the misdemeanor count and one year of supervised release. I was taken off of home confinement. He ordered me to continue therapy and I was now under the supervision of the U.S. Probation Office. I could use the computer but I wasn't allowed to look at any pornography and my computer was going to be monitored by Probation. It was weird because I had been acquitted of all of the pornography related stuff, but I wasn't going to argue.

Being off of home confinement felt great. The first thing I did was walk Dudley. For the next couple of weeks I would go out just for the sake of going out. I would just wander around aimlessly, soaking in the sounds of the city. I was able to go out with friends again. I wasn't allowed to leave Queens without permission from my probation officer, but he was never a problem for me. I actually got along fairly well with him. One of my requirements for probation was that I had to get a job. Studying for and taking the LSAT wasn't good enough, so I started to send out some resumes.

I must have applied for around twenty jobs that I was well over-qualified for, but I didn't hear back from anyone. It seemed that no one was willing to give me a chance considering my recent history, and that was frustrating. Although I had been cleared, I was still dealing with the ripple effects of the case.

My probation officer suggested an organization that helps people with criminal records find work. So I went, but it didn't really help me. They were teaching people how to write resumes, how to dress for job interviews, and all kinds of other things that I wasn't having a problem with. My problem was that companies would Google my name and see "Cannibal Cop" articles.

Towards the end of the first week with the organization, I

caved and asked someone for help. I called an old friend, explained what was going on, and he gave me a job right away working for his construction company. Gino wondered why I didn't ask him sooner, but I have never been the kind of guy who asks for help. I didn't know anything about construction but I was more than willing to learn.

My mother used to work for that company so I already knew most of the people there. Despite all of the hoopla still surrounding me, nobody there has ever treated me any differently and I've never felt like people were judging me in any way. I feel completely normal there, and it was a step in the right direction for me mentally. I could just be Gil again.

The prosecutors went forward with their appeal, and we cross-appealed the misdemeanor conviction. We felt good about both, but there was still the possibility that the Court of Appeals could reinstate the guilty verdict for the conspiracy count and then I would be back at square one. It was tough to live like that. On one hand, I tried to move on with my life, study for the LSAT and try to learn something new every day at work, but at the drop of a hat I could end up back in prison. Additionally, the appeal kept me from pursuing visitation with my daughter.

Though things were mostly okay, I was dealing with some collateral damage. I had frequent nightmares about being back in prison, and I wasn't able to sleep with the bedroom door closed. Closing the door made me feel confined. I was also dealing with some paranoia issues. I would hear a car driving down the block around two or three in the morning and would run to the window to try and see who was out there. I thought that the government was watching me.

At least I was working again and I was going out without

being recognized. I thought that it might be cool to start dating again, so late one night I signed up for Match.com. I had no idea how to explain my past to a potential date, or when the right time to explain it was. When I talked to people I trusted about it, no one ever really had an answer either. So I figured, I'll roll the dice and see what happens.

What happened was, a few days later, I was back on the front page of the New York Post under the headline "Hungry For Love." I don't know how they found it, but they did and they completely blew me up. I wasn't as embarrassed as I thought I would be. My dad was pretty pissed but he got over it. My mom kind of rolled her eyes. I was deathly afraid of Julia though. She told me to keep a low profile. Just as I was thinking about Julia, she texted me.

"I'm sorry. This too shall pass," she said.

I called her up and she was surprisingly okay with it. Once I told her I was fine, we were able to laugh about it. She said, hey, at least it's out there now. I was out of the house when I talked to her, but I looked forward to getting home and seeing if I had any messages. Unfortunately, Match.com deleted my profile. I was okay with the New York Post article, but Match.com deleting my profile really ticked me off.

The story was picked up all over the place and I had media stake outs in front of my house again. Daniel Engber contacted me and asked if it was okay if he wrote an article basically saying "Leave him the hell alone, he's been cleared." I told him he could do it, and he wrote a great article backing me up. This whole episode was an important lesson. People were interested in everything that I did.

Dating wasn't dead though. A couple of weeks later I was

browsing around Facebook and checking out "People I May Know," and I recognized one of the names. It was one of the Fordham Law students who worked on my case and visited me in prison. I sent her a message thanking her, then, she wrote a really beautiful message back saying that she had thought about me from time to time and wondered how I was moving on with my life. We exchanged phone numbers, agreed to meet, and we hit it off for a passionate few months. It was so nice to just be able to be myself and not have to worry about when the right time was to tell someone about my past. She knew everything, and she was fine being with me.

There started to be some press about Erin's upcoming documentary. It was going to premiere at the Tribeca Film Festival. I was looking forward to it more than anything. People were going to watch this documentary and finally get the truth about the case. Finally, my name was going to be cleared.

I had a meeting at the HBO office in Manhattan with Erin, Sheila Nevins who runs HBO Documentaries, and some of the producers. I thanked them all for the opportunity to tell my story, and we talked about the logistics of the premiere night. They were giving me ten tickets for family and friends. There was going to be a Q & A panel after the screening and they wanted me to participate. I didn't have a problem with that. They also wanted me to do some press afterward. I would have to talk to Julia, but I wanted to help these people out any way that I could, especially after everything they were doing for me.

The day before I was going to see a pre-screening, on my birthday, Erin texted me and said that she was very excited for me to see the documentary. She kept up her act until the very last day.

A couple of hours later, I read an article that appeared in The Hollywood Reporter. They interviewed Erin about the documentary. One quote really struck me, and made me very wary:

"When he was in prison, it was so easy to say he was innocent. When he got out of prison, certain inconsistencies appeared, and when I presented them to him, he couldn't really answer me," Erin was quoted saying in the article.

I immediately texted her and asked for an explanation. To my recollection, she had never approached me with an inconsistency that I couldn't answer. It took her a couple of hours to respond, but when she did, it was a bullshit company line about journalism boundaries. My lawyers all saw the quote too, and they were concerned.

The next day my lawyers and I were at HBO to watch a screening of the movie before it premiered at Tribeca the next day. Sheila Nevins and the producers were also there with Erin. It was an utter disaster, and it became abundantly clear that Erin played me. The whole thing was a long con. After it was over, I voiced my displeasure and said that it was nowhere close to an accurate representation of what happened, and nowhere close to what Erin said it was going to be. Sheila said she understood, but they couldn't make a "propaganda fluff piece."

But what about the truth? The documentary made no mention of the fact that I graduated from the University of Maryland and Erin spun the trip to Maryland when I had brunch with Kate into this creepy occurrence just like the U.S. Attorney's office did. Erin made it look like a legitimate overt act. The letter from Hadassa Waxman where she blatantly lied to

Judge Gardephe? Nowhere to be found. Neither were the text messages between Kathleen and I that gave the accurate depiction of our happy relationship. The bail hearings weren't covered at all, and neither was the potential perjury in the grand jury hearing, nor the actual provable perjury in Agent Foto's sworn statement.

A lot of truth was left out, and at the same time she elevated the government's case. Then there were all of the stupid scenes of me cooking, and cheesy footage of me in a dark room with artificial sound effects to make it look and sound like I was typing on a computer when in reality, I was doing nothing more than watching TV.

I read a lot of feedback after the documentary aired, and people were perplexed that I never mentioned my daughter. The thing is, I did. I talked a lot on camera about how much I missed her and how heartbroken I was that she was forced to grow up without her father, but something like that wasn't important enough for Erin. A shot of me eating a burrito was much more up her alley.

There were also no inconsistencies from me in the documentary. She never approached me with anything that could be construed as an inconsistency, so her quote in the Hollywood Reporter article was a ploy to get some eyeballs on her amateurish movie. I hated it and I was crushed. To her credit, Julia never gave me the "I told you so" speech. She said that it wasn't terrible and that she was more disappointed in Erin than anything. She was on board with my feeling that Erin betrayed us.

The next day I informed HBO that I was not going to be at the premiere, and neither was my family. They asked me to reconsider and I told them that I wouldn't. I wasn't going to appear there and support this severe misrepresentation of my case. It got even worse over the next couple of weeks. Erin did interview after interview and those confirmed to me that she was a pathological liar. I couldn't speak to the media so I couldn't refute anything. I was under strict orders from Julia not to voice my displeasure over the documentary. I think Erin knew that, so she went wild.

In one interview, she said that in the days after the premiere she kept trying to call me, but I was not returning her calls. She actually never called me once. I texted her and asked her why the hell she would lie about that. She apologized and called the person who interviewed her and asked for that quote to be removed. In another interview, she said that she had wanted to do a "horror documentary." In another, she said she had wanted to make a documentary where half of the people would walk out saying that they thought I would have murdered women, and half of the people would walk out saying that they did not think I would have done it.

Does anyone think that a person in my situation, still potentially facing life in prison, would voluntarily sign up for a horror documentary? Or would I voluntarily give the go ahead for a documentary that left the outcome 50/50? Of course not. She was also speaking for me during some of these interviews. "Gil felt" this, and "Gil wanted" that. I e-mailed HBO and asked them to get her to please refrain from speaking for me, but it continued.

I hated seeing her get all of this praise for gaining my cooperation. It was like, "Oh my gosh, David Carr's daughter got this huge story with the Cannibal Cop! What a great job! How did she get him to cooperate?" It absolutely made me sick. She got my cooperation by selling me a fairytale and then pulling the rug out from under me.

It severely depressed me and I basically went into hiding for a week. With the permission of my probation officer, I left town for a few days and spent some time with my family in Connecticut. I was able to keep current on Erin's interviews because she posted most of them on her Twitter account. After nearly every interview, I complained to HBO and eventually Erin blocked me.

I was more embarrassed and afraid to show my face in public after the documentary than I was when I was acquitted and released from prison. Judge Gardephe's ruling left no doubt as to my innocence. Erin's flimflam left the outcome of my case basically 50/50, and some people who watched it could think that I was on the verge of committing a murder.

I was so out of sorts for so long that I completely stopped studying for the LSAT and ended up bombing it. Eventually, either HBO got tired of hearing from me or they agreed that Erin was not upfront and honest with me about what she was going to do with the documentary, so they gave me $5,000 to shut me up, even though I wasn't supposed to be paid for my participation. It was a meager amount compared to what I am sure they made by exploiting me, but I wasn't going to complain about it, because it was certainly more than I had ever expected. In the long run, HBO ended up hiring Erin to do more work for them, which also disappointed me. They knew how unhappy I was because Erin had not been entirely forthcoming and honest with me, but that didn't seem to matter at all to them.

Ultimately, after a couple of very difficult months, just like the Match.com media fiasco, life went on and that bad period passed. Some people who saw the documentary and reached the right conclusion despite Erin's shenanigans were reaching out to me on social media and offering their support. That helped immensely. Still, I will forever regret trusting Erin.

As far as the case, it was dragging out just like it did while it was in Judge Gardephe's hands. There was an oral argument before the Court of Appeals. One of the judges on the panel compared my case to a fictional case involving leprechauns delivering cocaine from the moon, so things seemed like they would work out, but day after day passed with the prospect of facing a new trial and ending up back in prison still hanging over me. When I was having a tough day and I was really worried, I would read Judge Gardephe's ruling again and I would calm down. As everything was dragging out, my daughter was still growing up without her father. My family was also completely shut out of her life and it was beyond heartbreaking.

I had completed my year of supervised release and the case was still pending. I was no longer under the supervision or monitoring of the U.S. Probation Office and I was able to do whatever I wanted again. I could freely travel, and I could freely surf the web. If I wanted to, I could go back to the Dark Fetish Network. I didn't, but I would occasionally look at BDSM pornography again.

At my job, I began taking an interest in construction estimating but I also wanted to experience a job site. Two days a week, I was out of the office and learning under Mike Napoli, one of the project managers. It was like learning a new language, but I tried to pick up something new every day. On a random Thursday in December of 2015, I was in the trailer at the job site, filing something away around ten in the morning. My cell phone in my pocket beeped twice. It was Julia texting me.

"We won!"

"Everything!"

And just like that, without any warning, it was all over.

AFTERWARD

Not only did the Court of Appeals uphold Judge Gardephe's ruling on the conspiracy acquittal, but they overturned the misdemeanor as well. I am now 100% exonerated, cleared of all criminal wrongdoing. In their ruling, the Court of Appeals wrote:

"We are loath to give the government the power to punish us for our thoughts and not our actions. That includes the power to criminalize an individual's expression of sexual fantasies, no matter how perverse or disturbing. Fantasizing about committing a crime, even a crime of violence against a real person whom you know, is not a crime. We do not believe that the prosecution satisfies the proof beyond a reasonable doubt standard by relying upon a distinction [between the 'fantasy' chats and the 'real' chats] that is untethered to reason or common sense."

It took me awhile, but I realize now how important the first half of that quote is. Early on, I was more passionate about the prosecutorial misconduct in this case but, over time, I have come to realize how important the "thought crime" angle is, and how it relates to all of us in society. How full would our prisons be if the government could jail us based on our thoughts, or even upon Google searches when not accompanied by any actions? How many people do you know that have fantasized about doing something that was against the law?

I understand and fully support conspiracy laws. People who

are planning legitimate crimes, especially violent crimes, need to be stopped before they succeed. Law enforcement should not have to wait for the crime to occur. With my case though, it should have been absolutely clear that I was not involved in a real kidnapping conspiracy. This case involved a "conspiracy" without any co-defendants or any kind of undercover FBI sting whatsoever. I was on trial for a conspiracy with myself. They didn't just swoop in and arrest me immediately either. They had me under surveillance for 30 days and literally didn't find anything. Most likely, I probably just had a bad draw and had very rookie or doggedly determined agents assigned to my case.

I think we would all agree that people should not be jailed for thoughts. But when, if ever, does a thought cross the line and become a crime? There needs to be some action, obviously, but how much action? I am not sure what the answer is. That is for smarter people than me to figure out, but I am hopeful that my story is a good starting point and I pray that what happened to me doesn't ever happen to anyone else.

Freedom of speech is our right as Americans under the First Amendment, but it is not always easy for people to defend. It's one thing to laugh and defend someone who wants to say that the sky is purple, but it's a whole different thing to defend someone like me. I never asked for people to support and defend my sexual fantasies, and I am not asking for people to like me and be my friend, but I do hope that the people who are most disgusted and repulsed by the things that I wrote can still conclude that I should not have been thrown in prison for the rest of my life for just thinking and pretending.

Since I have now been completely cleared, I am suing the feds. I spent twenty-one months – six hundred and sixteen days - in prison for a crime I did not commit, and I am thankful that I found an attorney to represent me in my fight for compensation for the time that I lost and the emotional suffering I endured, especially while in solitary confinement for seven months. I am also filing a complaint of judicial misconduct against Hadassa Waxman. The amount of lying she did was astounding, and she should not be allowed to get away with that, especially in a case that involved potentially sending a defendant to prison for life.

I wrote a lot about the lies the prosecutors told. All anyone has to do is read the whole case for the proof. It is crystal clear. Unfortunately, I am not the only innocent person who has spent time in prison. Something needs to change in the justice system. In my opinion, nothing would be better than for prosecutors to be held accountable and penalized when, like in my case; it can be proven that they intentionally misled the Court.

I have continued seeing the same therapist every week as a private patient. He has been instrumental to my personal growth and in adjusting to a new life with the "Cannibal Cop" stigma attached to my name. I haven't continued with him hoping that he would say a magic word and then poof, I would not be aroused by those unusual fetishes anymore. I still very much have my sexual fantasies. They are part of who I am, but they do not define me or the person I am in real life. Unfortunately, I became somewhat of a poster boy for sexual fetishes and thought crimes and I wouldn't wish this on my worst enemy. I don't think anyone out there would let their deep, secret fetishes and fantasies be known if they didn't want to.

In a way though, it has been somewhat liberating to have all of this out there, but I still wish I had my old life back. I wish

I was still married to Kathleen, and I wish I were still with the NYPD. I wish I could have heard my daughter's first words and I wish I could have seen her grow up and learn the kinds of things she is interested in. For me, the most heartbreaking part of this whole case is that my daughter has been forced to grow up in a home without her father. I have no idea how I will eventually explain all of this to her, but I know I will figure it out.

I am still in the process of pursuing visitation privileges. That is my most important legal battle at the moment. My family sporadically wrote letters to her and her family while I was in prison, but they were ignored. My family's suffering and being shut out of my daughter's life hurts me even more. They did nothing to deserve that kind of cold-hearted treatment from my daughter's family in Nevada. We have no idea what my daughter even looks like.

Kathleen is saying that she still believes that I am a threat and she is fighting me being a part of my daughter's life, although she has no problem taking my money. I also think it is possible that she is forced to keep the narrative going that I am a threat who is incapable of being a parent since she lied on the witness stand about our relationship, so changing her tune would essentially be her admitting that she committed perjury. Whatever the case may be, reconciliation with Kathleen is impossible and I am okay with that now. It will never happen. I am sorry that I never came clean with her about my sexual fantasies, and I'll always regret the emotional pain it caused her and how it forever drove us apart. I am fiercely motivated to rebuild my life, because if I don't, then Hadassa Waxman, Randall Jackson, and Agent Foto still win. I will not let that happen. I am still working for the same construction company and I've learned a lot about the industry. I am forever grateful to Gino and his brother Johnny for the opportunity they gave me. I've reconnected with more of my old NYPD colleagues and although I am still occasionally upset at the lack of support they showed, I understood the spot they were in and it's mostly water under the bridge.

I remain in contact with Julia. I could never, ever forget everything that she did for me. I don't know if my trial was the most stressful moment of her life. If it was, then we're forever connected through some of our darkest days.

Julia and the rest of the federal defenders did outstanding work, but the decision still rested with Judge Gardephe. Federal judges don't swoop down from the heavens and sit on trials. They are men and women too. They are human beings with their own thoughts and emotions and I have to think that Judge Gardephe at times wondered what would happen if he ordered my release and I brutally murdered someone. Of course I wouldn't, but to his credit he stuck to the law. Leaving the jury's verdict would have been the easy thing to do, but he had the wisdom and the courage to do the right thing. I hope that life takes him and his family as far as he wants to go.

Elsewhere, I found out that my friend who retired has his own BDSM fantasies that he is into. In all of the hours we worked together, we had never talked to each other about that. I've confided a lot in him, including when I started to get messages from women on social media who were not only fascinated by my case but were turned on by my sexual fantasies. He told me about a sex shop in Queens.

Before I hooked up with one of those women, after vetting her for weeks, of course, I went into the sex shop. The woman behind the counter recognized me right away.

"Oh my God, it's you! I just saw the documentary about your case last night!"

She was really cool, and after I vented about the documentary and how it wasn't an accurate representation of what happened, she showed me around. I felt really comfortable there with her. I told her that I was going to meet up with a girl who wanted to have some fun with some bondage toys and she gave me two thumbs up and said she was so happy for me. So I bought some toys and spent a weekend with a girl who was fine with me tying her up. We talked about hard lines and safe words, and then we had some fun. I cuffed her, gagged her, blindfolded her, and whipped her just to start. She loved every second of it, and I was having a lot of fun too. We engaged in consensual adult behavior with safe words, and we both had a wonderful time. She's a funny, smart, and just brilliant young woman who is passionate about the law. Although she is younger than I am, I learned a lot from her. She is very open about her own sexual kinks and lives an amazing, successful life. We are absolutely still in touch.

One of my fears when I was released from prison was that I wouldn't be accepted anywhere. I thought that I would be seen as a pariah and a potential homicidal maniac. With time, I now know that I am not destined to a life of loneliness. I'll meet another woman, someone who accepts everything about me, and I'll settle down again.

Until then, I am doing everything a normal person does. I refuse to hide from this, and I've come to accept the "Cannibal Cop" part of my life. It was a nightmare, but I now know who my true friends and family are and I have a new appreciation for life. I love everyone who stuck with me and supported me through the most difficult days.

Not everything is peachy though. I still sleep with the bedroom door open and I still have intense nightmares. I still go through an occasional bout of depression because I have lost everything that I had known. I am active on social media and get the occasional trolling and public shaming, but I try not to let it bother me. Most of the time I am okay with people busting my chops, but people also need to understand that I am still dealing with a lot of stuff and when I am having one of those really bad days, they need to back off.

I wish I was known for something better, but it is, what it is. Life goes on. I have no choice.

The issue of thought crime is one reason why I wanted to write a book about my case. I also felt that I had an obligation to myself and the people who wholeheartedly believed in my innocence to, once and for all, get the full, accurate version of events out there, because Erin and HBO failed miserably.

There is one more reason why I wrote this book, but I struggled whether or not to include this. At the time this book is released, my daughter (whose name I intentionally left out throughout the book) still will not know who her father is. I am working on rectifying that. She is still very young, and just starting school, but one day she will be old enough to look into what happened with her father on her own. This will happen whether or not a family court judge grants me the right to reunite with my daughter and be a part of her life. I want to give my daughter, ten or fifteen years from now, the chance to read my side of the story.

Some people might think, "How can a father want his daughter to read a graphic book like this?" I understand that view, but when she looks into all of this on her own, she will see that graphic stuff in news articles anyway. Those news articles that she would see, and anything else that is mainstream and easily available, do not cover the lying and misconduct by law enforcement.

So, yes, my precious daughter, I wanted you to know my side of the story and up to and including the release of this book, there hasn't been a day when I haven't thought about you and felt emptiness in my heart because we're not together and it's my fault. I love you every single day.

Me with a really fun street band in Portland, Maine

Took a helicopter tour of New York City. I am not a good flier, but this was awesome

A night out on the town

South Street Seaport in New York City

The Brooklyn Bridge is in the background

My two dogs sleeping in late one morning. Tyson and Dudley

Let's go Yankees!

See even more at:
http://wbp.bz/tc

More True Crime You'll Love From WildBlue Press

BOGEYMAN: He Was Every Parent's Nightmare by Steve Jackson
"A master class in true crime reporting. He writes with both muscle and heart." (Gregg Olsen, New York Time bestselling author). A national true crime bestseller about the efforts of tenacious Texas lawmen to solve the cold case murders of three little girls and hold their killer accountable for his horrific crimes by New York Times bestselling author Steve Jackson. *"Absorbing and haunting!"*(Ron Franscell, national bestselling author and journalist)

wbp.bz/bogeyman

REPEAT OFFENDER by Bradley Nickell
"Best True Crime Book of 2015" (Suspense Magazine) A "Sin City" cop recounts his efforts to catch one of the most prolific criminals to ever walk the neon-lit streets of Las Vegas. *"If you like mayhem, madness, and suspense, Repeat Offender is the book to read."*(Aphrodite Jones, New York Times bestselling author)

wbp.bz/ro

DADDY'S LITTLE SECRET by Denise Wallace
"An engrossing true story." (John Ferak, bestselling author of Failure Of Justice, Body Of Proof, and Dixie's Last Stand) Daddy's Little Secret is the poignant true crime story about a daughter who, upon her father's murder, learns of his secret double-life. She had looked the other way about other hidden facets of his life - deadly secrets that could help his killer escape the death penalty, should she come forward.

wbp.bz/dls

BODY OF PROOF by John Ferak
"A superbly crafted tale of murder and mystery."– (Jim Hollock, author of award-winning BORN TO LOSE) When Jessica O'Grady, a tall, starry-eyed Omaha co-ed, disappeared in May 2006, leaving behind only a blood-stained mattress, her "Mr. Right," Christopher Edwards, became the suspect. Forensic evidence gathered by CSI stalwart Dave Kofoed, a man driven to solve high-profile murders, was used to convict Edwards. But was the evidence tainted? A true crime thriller written by bestselling author and award-winning journalist John Ferak.

wbp.bz/bop

Printed in Great Britain
by Amazon

71209378R00139